LATRE'

The Art Of Traveling Cheap

MIDNITE DAKOTA
PUBLISHING

To my mother,
who spent her last on "unnecessary" cruises just to give me
memories,
who showed me the ocean and slipped a travel bug in my chest.
You gave me wonder, you gave me motion, you gave me the world.
Thank you.
Forever your Shuge, your Fat Fat, forever my entire heartbeat, my
partner in crime.

Contents

How It Started

I love spending money, but not on traveling. Ironically, traveling is one of my favorite things to do. I've been all over: Aruba, the Bahamas, Costa Rica, the Dominican Republic. I've zigzagged the United States from Las Vegas to New York to the Smoky Mountains in Tennessee. So how does someone who hates spending money on travel manage to travel this much? Easy. Travel hacks, but not the tired ones you've heard a thousand times. I mean real hacks: beating the system, or better yet, making the system work for you.

This book is my playbook. It's the guide I wish I had years ago. I've spent years and countless hours doing the research so you don't have to, testing ideas on real trips, keeping what works, trashing what doesn't. The tips and tricks here come from my own wins and my own mistakes and none of them require a credit card points PhD. So sit back, roll a Jay, grab a pen and a notebook, and let's get ready to take flight.

Truth is, this book didn't start once. It started, stopped, restarted, again and again, because that's how life goes. I've always loved to travel, and I've always hated spending money, on anything. For a long time, my money habits were trash. I'd get mad when bills came due, and instead of paying them like a responsible adult, I'd act like avoiding them was a plan. I bought cars I didn't pay for and woke up to empty parking spots like I was the victim. I moved and thought that meant the bills couldn't find me. Spoiler: they always could. I talk about that old, terrible lifestyle in another book titled "What Happens When You Don't Pay Your Bills", and everything that came with it. I've learned from those mistakes. I still hate spending money, I just use it as a tool now.

I've been figuring out vacation cheat codes since I was nineteen, but it didn't turn into a real passion until COVID hit. Yeah, I was one of those people traveling during the pandemic. Flights and rooms were stupid cheap. I moved back in with my mom to help her and to cut costs. I was freelancing, living in the basement, and heavy into the stock market, up early for the opening bell, dabbling in options, stacking dividends, trying to make the numbers move while the world stood still.

One day the Wi-Fi cut out, prepaid, temperamental, you know the vibe, right when I had a $200 options play heating up. I grabbed my laptop, flew to the nearest McDonald's, jumped on the free Wi-Fi, and braced for the worst. Instead, the play exploded. I was up more than $700, sitting under a plastic menu board with a lukewarm coffee. I cashed out and thought, if I can make $700 at McDonald's, what could I make doing this from somebody's beach?

So I used the little travel knowledge I had and booked a week in the Dominican Republic: about $480, all-inclusive! That means unlimited food, unlimited liquor, a resort full of sunshine and beautiful women. While I was still at that McDonald's, another options play went on a bull run. Seven minutes after I spent $480, I'd made over $900. That was the moment. I booked my flight as cheap as I could, this was peak COVID pricing, around $364 round-trip. All in, I spent about $840 for seven days in the DR and made more than I spent before my order number was even called. I haven't looked back since.

Since then, I've done the hours and the miles. I've traveled the world for less and built real memories inside and outside the country. I don't just research this stuff, I live it, so I can write it down and hand it to you. Traveling is worth it. The things you see, the people you meet, the moments that rewire your brain, it's all worth it. And you don't need a massive budget to claim it. Honestly, you don't need much of a budget at all if you move smart.

People love to call credit card rewards "travel hacks." Nah. That's not hacking, that's just using a bank's coupon book. What about folks who don't have or don't want a credit card? Or the ones like me who wrecked their credit and couldn't get one even if they tried? I've got you. The pages ahead are real hacks for real life. Traveling cheap isn't hard. It isn't about collecting miles or worshiping points. And it definitely isn't a secret.

What it is, is an art, an art form. And I'm here to share it with you.

Welcome to The Art of Traveling Cheap.

Where I've Been

I don't just talk travel, I've done it. Here's a snapshot of places I've actually touched down in:

International

- Belize
- Bahamas
- Costa Rica
- Dominican Republic
- Aruba
- Cozumel, Mexico
- Half Moon Cay
- Thailand
- Japan
- UK
- Paris
- Netherlands
- Australia
- Russia

United States

- Las Vegas, Nevada
- Smoky Mountains, Tennessee
- Richmond, Virginia

- Washington, DC
- New York City, New York
- Miami, Florida
- Orlando, Florida
- Atlanta, Georgia
- Atlantic City, New Jersey
- Ocean City, Maryland
- National Harbor, Maryland
- Baltimore Harbor, Maryland
- Williamsburg, Virginia
- Philadelphia, Pennsylvania
- Pittsburgh, Pennsylvania
- Hershey, Pennsylvania
- Norfolk, Virginia
- Smithfield, Virginia
- North Carolina
- South Carolina

Cheap Flights

Flights usually eat the biggest chunk of your budget. They don't have to. Cheap flights aren't about luck; they're about strategy. Most people think scoring a deal is about being in the right place at the right time, but really, it's about how you search and how flexible you're willing to be.

The #1 mindset shift: flexibility beats stubbornness. If you only look at one date, one airport, and one airline, you're volunteering to get ripped off. The more settings you're willing to adjust, the cheaper your flight gets. Think of travel like playing a game with sliders:

- Dates are sliders, not stones.
- Airports are options, not obligations.
- One itinerary is a starting point, not the final answer.

Or an even better example could be thinking of finding a flight like finding a girlfriend on tinder. The more you change your preferences the more options you will get. Once you start treating flights like a puzzle instead of a fixed price tag, you stop searching like a tourist and start hunting like a pro.

Now, here's the truth: you don't need fifty apps or to scroll endlessly for hours. You need a handful of tools you know how to drive with precision.

Google Flights is your control room. Put in your home airport, set flexible dates, and pull up the explore map. You'll see the whole world's prices laid out in one sweep. Move the sliders for departure and return by a day or two and watch the fares drop. Click into the date grid and price graph, this feature alone exposes which week is a scam and which week is gold. Toggle on price tracking and let deals come to you while you live your life.

Skyscanner and Kayak are your backup hitters. They catch budget carriers and odd combinations Google sometimes misses. Skyscanner especially shines for connector loopholes, routes where splitting a trip into two legs is way cheaper than nonstop. A lot of people skip this step. Don't. Sometimes flying into one hub and then connecting yourself with a budget carrier saves you hundreds.

Deal alerts & newsletters are your early warning system. Subscribing to a list like Going.com (Scott's Cheap Flights) or setting up Google Alerts for cities you care about is one of the smartest moves you can make. Mistake fares and flash sales can vanish in hours, so being on the list gives you a head start while everyone else is still scrolling Instagram.

And don't sleep on package providers. Sites like GateOne-Travel.com sometimes drop insane packages that cost less than the flight alone. I've seen deals like 6 days in Milan with flights included for $500. If you were only searching airline sites, you would've missed it. Same goes for FlightConnections.com, which maps out all routes between airports so you can see hidden hubs that might unlock better fares.

The goal is simple, build your baseline search in Google Flights, sanity-check it with Skyscanner/Kayak, skim newsletters, and cross-check packages. Book where the total price (after baggage, fees, and extras) is lowest. That flow alone will save you more money than most people ever realize is possible.

Airports, Dates & Trip Shapes

One of the most powerful levers you can pull on price is your choice of airports. Everyone defaults to their nearest big hub, but that's lazy traveling. Sometimes the best move is to drive an hour or two out of your way. Add up gas, tolls, and parking, then compare it to the fare savings. More often than not, the "inconvenient" airport ends up saving you $100 to $300. Don't be afraid to drive.

Connector flights are another overlooked weapon. Most people search nonstop because they don't want the hassle, but if you don't mind layovers, you can often cut the price dramatically. A single stop can slash hundreds off an international ticket. If time isn't your main priority, build your trip around connectors instead of paying extra for nonstops.

Now let's talk timing. Everybody asks: "When's the best day to fly?" The answer: midweek wins. Tuesday, Wednesday, and even Saturday tend to be cheaper because most travelers stick to the Friday–Sunday pattern. Airlines know the herd, and they price accordingly. Break away from the herd and you'll pay less. A lot of folks fly to see family during the holidays. I say don't do it... Ask: "How much do you even like your family?" Is the price/crowds worth it?

Another overlooked hack: fly on the actual holiday. Everyone scrambles to leave the day before Thanksgiving or Christmas, which makes those days the most expensive. But flights on Thanksgiving morning or Christmas Day? Dirt cheap. The plane will be half empty because everyone's already at Grandma's house. If you're willing to sacrifice part of the holiday morning, you'll save big.

The same applies to holiday windows. If you can travel well before or well after the peak days, prices drop. Go the week before Christmas or the week after New Year's, and you'll see the difference instantly.

Seasonality matters too. The cheapest months to fly internationally are usually September, October, and November. Kids are back in school, summer vacation demand is over, and the holiday rush hasn't kicked in yet. That dead space is where airlines quietly slash fares to keep planes full. Travelers who don't know this keep overpaying in July, while smart travelers enjoy the same destinations for half the price in the fall.

Finally, stop thinking only in terms of round-trips. Airlines love to lock you into one ticket, but sometimes two separate one-ways, even on different airlines, beat the round-trip price. Other times, an open-jaw itinerary (flying into one city and home from another) saves both money and backtracking. Some airlines even let you add a stopover for little to nothing, basically giving you two vacations for the price of one.

Flexibility with airports, dates, and trip shapes isn't glamorous advice, but it's where the real money is saved. Every time you expand your options, you cut the airline's ability to box you in at their price.

Budget Airlines & Bag Strategy

Budget airlines get a bad rap, and for good reason: they look cheap upfront but they'll nickel and dime you for everything. The secret is to treat them like vending machines. Every extra has a price tag, so only "buy" what you truly need.

Spirit and Frontier are the poster children of this model. Their fares look dirt cheap, sometimes $50 or less, but if you show up unprepared, you'll walk away having paid the same as a legacy airline with half the comfort. The hack is to fly ultra-light. Spirit's frequent-flyer program can actually be valuable if you know how to work it. Frontier even has an "all you can fly" summer or yearly pass that lets you book unlimited flights for a flat fee. If you live near one of their hubs and you're flexible, that pass can pay for itself in just a couple of trips.

On the international side, don't ignore budget carriers you've probably never heard of. Airlines like PLAY (Iceland), Icelandair, French Bee, ZIPAIR (Tokyo routes), and Norse Atlantic (out of Norway) run flights to the U.S. and Europe at prices legacy airlines rarely match. For under $200 one-way, you can cross the Atlantic, if you know how to pack smart. These airlines exist specifically to scoop up price-sensitive travelers. Take advantage of them.

Packing is where most people fail. Budget airlines live off bag fees. If your luggage is even slightly oversized, they'll charge you more than the flight cost itself. The fix? Pack lighter than you think. Measure your personal item bag so you know it passes their limits. Use compression bags to shrink your clothes and maximize space. Stick to multi-use outfits and don't overpack shoes.

Food is another hidden fee trap. In-flight meals cost ridiculous amounts, and most budget carriers don't even offer a free snack. Hack it by bringing your own. One of the oldest tricks in the book? Pack ramen noodles in your carry-on. Once you're onboard, just ask the flight attendant for hot water. Congratulations, you've got a warm meal at 30,000 feet for 50 cents. Bring your own snacks! You can bring food and drink on bored as long as it's completely sealed.

Another overlooked cost: seat selection. Airlines love to scare you into paying $25–$50 to lock in a seat. Truth is, if you don't care where you sit, skip it. You'll usually still get a regular seat assignment for free at check-in. Middle seat? Who cares. It's still the same plane going to the same place.

Here's the rule: don't give budget airlines any more money than you have to. If you know their game and come prepared, you'll walk away with dirt-cheap flights that stay dirt-cheap. If you don't, you'll bleed fees and end up paying the same as a full-service airline with none of the perks.

Timing, Rights, Rewards & Scams

People love to complicate flight deals with points, cards, and insurance. The truth is simpler: most of that stuff only helps if you play it perfectly. If you slip up even a little, the "deal" becomes a trap.

Points always lose value over time. Airlines devalue their loyalty programs every few years. That stash of 60,000 miles you've been hoarding? Worth less now than when you earned it. If you're going to use points, use them sooner rather than later. You should never go into debt just to earn them. Earning 2% back on a card that charges you 16% in interest makes zero sense. Don't pay $500 to save $20.

That's why I always say: cash is king. If you have the money to buy the flight outright, buy it. If you're using a credit card, pay it off in full. Otherwise, you're not traveling cheap, you're just building debt in the name of "rewards."

What about travel insurance? Honestly? It's not as useful as it used to be. I'd even call most of it a scam. Since COVID, airlines were forced to adjust their rules on cancellations and refunds. In many cases, you're already covered by law. Paying for "extra" insurance just gives you a false sense of security.

Here's what actually matters: your refund rights. If an airline cancels your flight, you are legally owed a refund within seven days. Not credit, not a voucher, a refund. Section 75 of the

Consumer Credit Act makes it even stronger: if you paid with a credit card, the card company is just as responsible for the service as the airline. That means if the airline plays games, your bank has to step up. Debit cards have similar protections, but with one catch, you need to show you made reasonable attempts to get your money back first. That's where emails come in. Always keep proof: unanswered emails, responses that dodge the issue, or screenshots of hidden fees. Documentation wins disputes. And don't forget, most people don't even know their rights. Surveys show about 75% of travelers don't realize airlines legally owe them cash when they cancel. That's how airlines get away with offering worthless vouchers instead. Don't be part of that 75%.

If You're in the U.K. vs. U.S.: Who Protects You?

U.K.

Law: Section 75 of the Consumer Credit Act

What it does: Makes your credit card company jointly liable with the merchant when a purchase goes wrong

Typical coverage: Purchases between £100 and £30,000 paid directly on a credit card

Use it for: Canceled flights where the airline refuses a lawful refund, undelivered services, or misrepresentation

Notes to know:

· It is for credit cards, not debit cards

13

- Paying through an intermediary can break the chain between you and the supplier
- This is a statutory right, separate from any "chargeback"

What to say to your card issuer:

"I am making a Section 75 claim for a flight service that was not provided. I paid on my credit card, the merchant has refused a refund, and the purchase value meets the Section 75 threshold. Please open a Section 75 claim rather than a voluntary chargeback."

What to keep on file: booking confirmation, evidence the flight was canceled or not provided, refund refusal in writing, and a timeline of your requests

U.S.

Law: Fair Credit Billing Act
   What it does: Gives you the right to dispute unauthorized or billing-error charges with your card issuer
   How you actually get your money back: Card-network chargebacks through your issuer
   Use it for: Services not provided, duplicate charges, or amounts you did not authorize
   Timing tip: File promptly once it shows on your statement and supply proof the service was not delivered
   What to say to your card issuer:

"I am disputing a charge for air travel that was not provided. The airline canceled or materially changed the itinerary and has not refunded me. Please process this as a services-not-provided dispute and advise what documentation you need."

What to keep on file: booking confirmation, notice of cancellation or significant schedule change, written refund request, the airline's response, and any applicable policy screenshots

U.S. Department of Transportation refunds

When DOT rules help: Flights to, from, or within the United States that the airline cancels or significantly changes

What you are owed: A refund to your original form of payment for the unused ticket and any fees for services you did not receive

Practical move: Ask the airline for a refund first. If they refuse, reference DOT refund rights in writing, then escalate to your card issuer with the same evidence

Finally, timing isn't just about refunds, it's about how you book in the first place. Booking early is almost always cheaper, especially before holidays. The closer you get to peak travel windows, the higher fares climb. Combine that with off-season travel (September–November) and midweek flights (Tuesday–Thursday), and you're stacking savings on top of savings.

Bottom line? Skip the gimmicks. Don't let airlines and banks convince you that insurance or rewards are the path to cheap travel. The real path is cash in hand, smart timing, and knowing your legal rights.

- Deal sources & alerts: The Flight Deal newsletter; Google Alerts for routes; Skyscanner "everywhere"/loophole searches; Google Flights Explore/price graph ("Google's board").
- OTAs & flash sales: GateOneTravel.com (ex: $500/6-day Milan), plus coupon sites (RetailMeNot) when they apply.
- Price patterns: Tuesday–Thursday rule; leave Tuesday / return Tuesday; extend by 1 day to drop fare; fly earlier in the day to reduce cancellation risk; avoid TSA's busiest days (Sun after Thanksgiving, Wed before).
- Airports & routes: Check smaller/alternate airports; consider connector flights.
- "Mystery travel" / flexible destination mindset (open to "anywhere" to chase price).
- Research helpers: Use ChatGPT for tailored recs/itineraries from your dates, diet, budget.

Regional Hacks Around the World

United States

Domestic flights are their own beast. If you want consistent wins, keep a few rules in mind:

- Southwest Airlines: Two free checked bags, no change fees. They don't show up on Google Flights, so you have to check them separately.
- Ultra-low-cost carriers (Spirit, Frontier, Allegiant):

They're dirt cheap if you pack to a backpack. Skip extras, skip seat selection, and you can fly roundtrip for less than a tank of gas.

- Companion passes: Southwest's Companion Pass is basically a cheat code. Earn it, and someone flies with you for free (just pay taxes) on every trip.

Europe

Flying in Europe can feel like playing on easy mode.

- Budget airlines dominate: Ryanair and EasyJet offer tickets for as low as $20. The catch? They're strict about bags. Measure your personal item down to the centimeter.
- Secondary airports: That $20 "Paris" flight might actually land you in Beauvais an hour from Paris. Always factor transfer costs.
- Trains vs. flights: Sometimes the train wins. Paris to London on Eurostar, for example, beats flying once you add in security, baggage, and airport transfers.

Asia

Asia is home to some of the cheapest flights in the world.

- AirAsia, Scoot, Cebu Pacific: Flights between countries can run $30–$50 if you're flexible.
- Hub strategy: Fly into a major hub like Bangkok or Singapore first, then bounce to smaller destinations with cheap regional airlines.
- Flash sales: Many Asian carriers run weekly or monthly deals. Sign up for newsletters and pounce fast.

Caribbean & Latin America

These regions are notorious for price swings, especially during holidays.

- Holiday surges: Flights around Christmas and New Year's are brutal. Book months in advance or skip the peak season.
- All-inclusive bundles: Sometimes the flight + hotel + food package is cheaper than the flight alone. Always crunch the numbers.
- Smaller regional airlines: Copa, Caribbean Airlines, and LATAM often drop prices that big U.S. carriers won't match.

The Spirit Almost-Scam

I once bought a $99 Spirit ticket thinking I was slick. At the airport, they tried to hit me with a $79 bag fee. I wasn't having it. I stuffed everything into a backpack and walked through sweating bullets, but it worked. That's when I realized: budget airlines only work if you know the rules better than they do.

Thanksgiving Trap

Another time, I thought I could outsmart Thanksgiving flights. Wrong. Prices were $800 for a one-hour domestic hop. I refused to pay, so I drove ten hours instead. Lesson learned: some peak travel windows aren't worth fighting.

The Free Upgrade

Not every story is pain. Once, I was polite to a gate agent while everyone else gave her attitude. The flight was oversold, and she bumped me to first class for free. That day, I learned kindness at the airport is underrated, sometimes it's the best hack of all.

The Hidden-City Trick

I tested hidden-city ticketing once (booking a flight with a layover in the city I actually wanted). It worked, saved me $200, but it's risky. You can't check bags, and airlines can flag you if you do it often. It's a last-resort hack, not an everyday tool.

The Flight Hacker's Checklist

Here's your playbook. Take a picture of it, print it, memorize it, whatever works. Run this list before every booking and you'll stop bleeding money.

Search Smart

- Run your first search on Google Flights.
- Use the date grid & price graph to compare.
- Turn on price tracking alerts.

- Cross-check Skyscanner, Kayak, and the airline's own site.

Play With Airports

- Check every departure airport within 2 hours of you.
- Look at secondary airports at your destination.
- Factor in transfer costs before deciding.

Flex Your Dates

- Fly Tuesday–Thursday whenever possible.
- Test flights on actual holiday dates.
- Consider traveling the week before or after peak holidays.
- Add one extra day if it saves hundreds.

Trip Shape

- Compare two one-ways vs. round-trip.
- Test open-jaw itineraries.
- Look for stopover deals, two trips in one.

Bag & Fee Strategy

- Pack to a personal item whenever possible.
- Prepay for bags online.
- Skip seat selection unless you care where you sit.
- Bring your own food, ramen noodles + hot water beats overpriced snacks.

Know Your Rights

- Refunds are owed within 7 days for cancellations.
- Section 75 protections apply if you book on a credit card.
- Keep emails as proof of disputes.

Bonus Moves

- Use points only if you pay cards in full.
- Compare bundles vs. booking separate.
- Sign up for newsletters like Going.com.

Cheap flights aren't luck. They're skill. Flexibility with airports, dates, and trip shapes puts you ahead of the herd. Knowing your rights keeps you from being scammed. And if you play the budget airline game smart, packing light, skipping extras, and traveling off-season, you'll travel more often for less money.

Stay flexible, stay prepared, and remember: the plane is the same whether you paid $800 or $180. Travel smart, and you'll always be the one who got the better deal.

Cheap Stays

The biggest mistake people make with lodging is deciding on the "when" and the "where" before they ever consider the price. Don't do that to yourself. If you stop being precious about dates and zip codes, the map opens and the math softens. Now, if you have to be at a specific place at a particular time, that's one thing, but if your goal is just to travel and get away, then be more open! Holidays aren't sacred; they're expensive. Two Tuesdays from now will treat you better than the Saturday every wedding guest wants. Flex even a little, and rooms you thought were out of reach start waving at you from the next tab over.

The second mistake is tunnel vision. When you only search one city or a single neighborhood, you trap yourself in a high-demand box. The cure is to start broad. Pick "any destination," tap the calendar view, and sort by the cheapest price first. On big booking sites, Expedia, Hotels.com, Kayak, Priceline, you'll sometimes see flash rates that look like typos, the kind of outlier that happens when a property wants heads in beds tonight. I've seen one-digit nightly rates pop up like Easter eggs. They don't last, and they're not guaranteed, but they exist often enough that it's worth the thirty seconds to check. The point isn't to chase a unicorn; it's to train your brain to look for value, not just preference.

Preferences still matter; you just fund them differently. If a certain brand makes you feel at home, lean into it. Pick a flag and join the loyalty program. You can book flights through all kinds of portals and still earn miles, but hotels are pickier. Many chains won't give you full points or elite credit if you book through third-party sites. That's why relationships pay. A simple rhythm works: hunt widely to learn the real floor price, then, when it's time to lock the stay, compare the chain's direct rate. If it's within striking distance, or if the chain is dangling a bonus for booking direct, go direct and let those nights stack up. Free breakfast, late checkout, and the "we found you a better room" conversation show up more often when your name has history.

Speaking of conversations, make them. Two days before you arrive, send a short email that says who you are, when you're showing up, and that you're excited to stay. Thank them for hosting you. If a special occasion is real, mention it. Don't write a script that sounds like a con; write like a human with manners. Then on the morning of check-in, call. Be kind, be specific, and ask a small question: Do you happen to have any complimentary upgrades available today? If the answer is no, you still set a tone that pays off in room placement, early keys, or just the kind of help you only get when someone remembers your name. It costs nothing to try, and it's the opposite of entitlement, it's participation.

Airbnbs are a tool, not a religion. They shine when you're a group of six or more, when you need a kitchen, or when you want a living room and a door that shuts after the kids fall asleep. Split across many people, a whole home can beat the nicest hotel in town on price per person. But when you're four or fewer, hotels start to win again, especially when you fold in things like housekeeping, security, on-site staff, and breakfast. Rate math is only step one; add cleaning fees, service fees, parking, and the time cost of check-in dance and you'll see why "cheaper" sometimes isn't. The right answer changes by trip, which is why you run the numbers every time.

Hostels, motels, and capsule hotels are the underrated third lane. A clean motel fifteen minutes outside the hot zone can feel like a miracle when downtown is charging like it's New Year's Eve. Pods and capsules scratch the novelty itch while keeping your wallet calm; you get privacy where it counts and you trade floor space you won't use for a price you'll brag about. Hostels aren't just bunk beds anymore; many offer private rooms with en-suite baths at prices that still undercut hotels. If you're open to community space and smart about your valuables, you'll meet the kind of travelers who turn a quiet night into a memory.

Couch-surfing stays live at the extreme low-cost edge. They're built on hospitality and trust, not room service. If you go this route, treat it like staying with a friend of a friend: read profiles deeply, pick verified hosts with many reviews, communicate clearly about arrival times and house rules, and bring the manners your grandmother taught you. The "price" you pay is being a good guest, leaving places cleaner than you found them, being quiet when people sleep, and remembering you're in someone's home. Done right, it's not just free; it's an exchange. You leave with a neighborhood's point of view money can't buy.

Distance is the oldest trick in the book and still one of the best. The farther you sleep from the postcard, the more your rate drops. This isn't about exiling yourself to the suburbs; it's about understanding the radius curve. Two stops on a frequent transit line can cut your price by a third. One freeway exit past the convention center can halve it on conference weeks. If you're renting a car anyway, a hotel near the edge of town with free parking can save more than it costs to fuel the extra miles. Pair that with a transit or ride share plan for your prime days and you get the best of both: sleep cheap, play central.

Budget for what you want, not what you wish. If a kitchen matters, because breakfast at home saves you $20 a day, own that and search for it as a non-negotiable. If you know you'll be out all day and only need a clean shower and a quiet bed, give yourself permission to book the simple place and pocket the difference. The trick is to decide on paper before the algorithm sells you an upgrade you won't use. The Hopper app fits here as a helper, not a decider. Let it watch rates, nudge you toward cheaper dates, and warn you when to book, but don't let a chart bully you into a stay that doesn't match your actual life.

There's a playful way to hunt: treat the entire metro area like a puzzle and see which pieces drop the total the most. Try your dates in reverse, arrive midweek, leave Sunday. Slide the trip by two days. Swap the city for the one fifty miles away that shares its airport but not its hotel taxes. Tell the search bar you're open to "everywhere," then sort by price. The exercise teaches you what the floor really is. Once you know that, you stop overpaying out of habit.

Loyalty isn't about worship; it's about leverage. Staying under the same brand family builds nights that turn into status, and status turns into better rooms, later checkout, and the occasional breakfast that changes the entire day's food math. But loyalty also has a cost if it traps you into paying more than a fair alternative just to chase points. I play it like this: aim for a soft loyalty path, enough stays to get the perks that matter to you, while giving yourself freedom to defect when a deal somewhere else is too good to ignore. Your job isn't to impress the brand; it's to take care of your trip.

Finally, remember that the cheapest bed is the one that fits the people coming. Airbnbs truly shine when you're rolling deep and want a kitchen table and a couch for late-night vibes. Hotels quietly win when you're a smaller crew that values on-site staff, luggage holds, and the ability to ask for help at 2 a.m. Motels carry the road-trip torch when all you need is easy parking and a ground-floor door. Pods deliver a futuristic, "I'm really doing this" grin for the price of a round of drinks. Keep your heart open, not set on one address. When you let the map surprise you, it usually does, with a cleaner room, a kinder rate, and a story worth telling.

One last nudge before we move on: call or email. Say hello. Be human. "We're excited to stay with you, any chance of a view or a quiet room?" costs nothing and pays more often than you think. And if the front desk says no to an upgrade, ask if there's a specific time you should check back. Rooms move. People cancel. It's free to ask, and sometimes that's the entire difference between a bed you tolerate and a stay you brag about.

Cheap stays don't come from one trick. They come from knowing how lodging makes money and then stepping neatly around the parts that don't serve you. The rate you see is only the first number; the bill you pay is the whole story. Once you learn to read that story, you stop getting surprised at the front desk.

Start by treating prices like a snapshot, not a truth. Rooms move every day, sometimes every hour. If your dates aren't locked, ride the calendar: arrive Tuesday, leave Friday, and watch the total sink compared to a weekend pair. If your dates are locked, book cleverly. I often start with a refundable rate that lets me sleep at night, then set a reminder to re-price the same room every few days. If it drops, I cancel and rebook in two taps. When rates move the wrong way, I'm still protected. Nonrefundable has a place, but only when the discount is meaningful and your plans are a rock. Thirty dollars saved isn't worth losing the entire reservation if your flight shifts.

The second lens is fees. Hotels love to keep them quiet: resort fees, destination fees, "facility" or "service" fees, parking, Wi-Fi, safe fees, coffee fees that look like a joke until they show up on checkout. Read the tax/fees line before you commit and, this part matters, screenshot it. If a pool is closed, the gym is under renovation, or breakfast "isn't available this month," that's your cue to ask for the fee to be removed or reduced. You're not arguing; you're aligning the bill with reality. "Since the advertised amenities are unavailable, could you waive the destination fee for my stay?" lands better than a rant and often gets a yes.

Third-party sites can be both hero and villain. They surface bargains and "secret rates" you'll never see on a chain's homepage. Use them to learn the floor price and to catch same-day outliers. But understand the trade-off: some brands won't honor loyalty perks or points on third-party bookings, and changes or issues must be handled through the site, not the front desk. My rhythm is simple: hunt wide, then compare the direct rate. If direct is close, and you care about points, upgrades, or a smoother problem-solving path, go direct. If a third-party rate wins by a mile, grab it, but keep a copy of the confirmation with the taxes and fees spelled out in plain English in case systems disagree at check-in.

Safety rides shotgun with price. A cheap room that steals your sleep is expensive by morning. Read reviews with a flashlight for the things that matter after dark: lighting in the lot, interior vs. exterior corridors, door hardware, neighborhood noise, and "felt safe walking in at 11 pm" from people who look like you or travel like you. In big cities, I like interior-corridor hotels with staffed lobbies; in smaller towns, I'll trade that for a tidy motel where my car is ten steps from the door. Rentals require a different checklist: smoke and carbon-monoxide detectors, clear house rules, no mention of "camera inside" (outside is common; inside is a no). If something feels off when you arrive, leave and call the platform. You can fix a bill. You can't fix a knot in your stomach. That knot can be prevented though.

Deposits and holds are where good trips get cash-flow cramps. Hotels place an incidental hold on your card at check-in, anywhere from $50 a night to a few hundred for the stay. On a credit card, that hold just limits available credit. On a debit card, it freezes your actual money for days after checkout. If you can, use a credit card at the desk and keep your debit card for ATMs and groceries. Ask what the hold amount is, when it releases, and whether you can reduce it by turning off room charging. If your budget is tight, that one question can be the difference between enjoying your first day and hunting for a cash deposit you didn't plan on.

Refundable vs. nonrefundable is a personality test masquerading as a rate code. If you're the kind of traveler who hates open loops, grab the nonrefundable only when the math is dramatic, think twenty percent or more, and when all the moving parts have already locked. Otherwise, be kind to your future self. Book the flexible rate, put a calendar alert for the property's cancellation deadline, and keep hunting. Often I'll split a four-night stay into two reservations: the first night nonrefundable (to secure the floor price I can live with), the remaining nights flexible (so I can pivot if something better appears). It's a simple way to hold value while keeping options.

Some savings are hiding in plain sight. Weekly and monthly discounts can turn an average nightly rate into a steal if your trip is long enough. On rental platforms, asking a host for a weekly special offer is normal; be polite, specific about dates, and offer to book immediately if they can meet a number. In hotels, corporate, AAA, government, senior, and mobile-only rates exist for a reason, if you qualify, use them. Price-match guarantees can work, but they take attention: you'll need a public, bookable lower rate for the exact same room type and dates. Submit the claim with screenshots while the rate is live and be patient; if it fails, you've still learned the property's true floor.

Check-in is where the human part starts. You've done the math; now you set the tone. I like to arrive with my screenshots in a "Stay" album, rate, fees, confirmation, and any closed-amenities notice. Something I used to do at the beginning of my cheap traveling journey was add everything to my notes. I would name the notes after the vacation destination and add any and all information surrounding it, email screenshots with confirmation numbers, flight information, and any other details I've secured.

Once you get to the front desk, lead with good energy: "Hey! I'm excited to be here." Then I ask a small, clear question that helps them help me: "Is there any chance of a quiet room away from the elevator?" or "If you have any complimentary upgrades available today, I'd really appreciate it." If the answer is no, it's no. Staff remember gracious people; the kindness has a way of coming back later in the stay.

Late checkout and early check-in are favors, not entitlements. Ask once at check-in; if the hotel is full, ask again in the morning before housekeeping assignments lock. At independent properties, I've had better luck explaining my day, "I've got a late flight; even an extra hour would help me a lot", than playing status chess. When they say yes, say thank you like you mean it, and tip appropriately where it makes sense. Hospitality is a relationship, not an algorithm.

Rentals have their own dance. Message the host two days before arrival with a friendly note and any specifics that avoid friction: ETA, parking questions, how they prefer you handle trash or keys. On arrival, do a three-minute photo walkthrough, stove, fridge, bathrooms, floors, and any pre-existing scuffs. Those photos protect everyone. If something's broken, report it immediately through the platform: "This was already like this when I arrived, just keeping us both covered." Hosts appreciate guests who communicate like partners.

There are nights when the cheapest thing you can do is leave. If a property fails the basic promises, no hot water, a door that won't latch, a room that hasn't been cleaned, document, ask for help once, and if the fix doesn't happen, escalate and relocate. The money will sort itself out; your time and safety won't. I've walked away from "deals" that cost me an hour of sleep just looking at them. The older I get, the cheaper rest becomes.

Put all of this together and the playbook is simple even if the page is long. Price is a moving target, book flexible when it serves you, commit when the discount is real. Fees are negotiable when amenities vanish, ask nicely and back it up with proof. Loyalty is leverage when used with a light touch, relationships beat rants. And check-in is your chance to turn a transaction into a stay you'll remember. Keep your screenshots, keep your manners, and keep your options open just long enough for the right room to land in your lap. That's how cheap lodging stops feeling like luck and starts feeling like a system you can run anytime you want.

Longer Stays, House-Sitting, Bedbug Checks, and the Mid-Trip Pivot

A cheap night is nice. A cheap week is strategy. The moment your stay stretches past four or five nights, the rules change in your favor if you know where to look. Hotels and hosts love reliable bodies in beds, and a longer booking is the most reliable kind. That's why weekly and monthly rates exist, the property spends less time cleaning, marketing, and checking people in, so the math lets them give you a break. You don't have to beg. You just have to ask like a pro.

I start by learning the real floor price. I'll price those dates across a few places, then write down what the average looks like. After that, I send a message that sounds like a human and not a haggler: "Hi! I love your place. I'm looking at [exact dates]. If I booked the full week today, could you do $X all-in?" Give a number that's fair for both of you and offer to book immediately if they can meet it. On rental platforms, keep every message inside the app. With hotels, I'll call the property directly during mid-shift, after the morning rush, before the afternoon arrivals, and ask for the manager on duty. Lead with the win for them as much as the win for you: fewer turnovers, one laundry instead of five, quiet guest who pays on time. The nicest discounts I've ever gotten arrived right after I explained how easy I'd be to host.

Sometimes the weekly rate is already published, hiding in a drop-down nobody clicks. Extended-stay hotels are built for this game. They give you kitchenettes, coin laundry, and a lobby that functions like a living room. If you're working remotely, those little extras end up saving more than the nightly rate suggests. They also attract regulars who treat the place like a neighborhood; you'll learn where the real groceries are and which takeout window is worth the walk. Monthly discounts can be dramatic if your schedule lets you settle in. Ask what "long-term" means in their system, some properties start the deal at seven nights, others at fourteen or thirty.

House-sitting is the elegant cousin of the extended stay. The arrangement is simple: you watch someone's home (and usually their pet) while they travel, and you live like a local in return. When it works, the savings are outrageous because your "rate" is responsibility instead of cash. The trade is honest, but it's not for dabblers. You need time, reliability, and manners. Read listings like a contract, ask clear questions about pet routines and house quirks, and plan to arrive a day early to learn the rhythm before the owners leave. I cook in their kitchen as if it were my grandmother's—cleaner when I'm done than when I started. If you're the kind of traveler who likes to inhabit a place rather than pass through it, house-sitting can turn a dream neighborhood into a practical address.

Hostels deserve a second look when you want privacy on a budget. The modern version isn't a backpacker free-for-all; it's a small ecosystem with private rooms, cowork tables, and kitchens. I book privates with en-suite bathrooms when I want quiet nights without hotel prices, and I let the shared kitchen cut my food bill in half. The staff usually know the city better than any brochure, and the bulletin board is a live feed of free concerts, walking tours, and volunteer gigs. If you're nervous about noise, ask for a room away from the bar or common area and bring earplugs just in case. You sleep better when you control the variables.

None of this matters if the bed itself betrays you. Bedbugs don't care how much you paid or how pretty the lobby looks. The check takes two minutes and can save a week of headaches. I walk in, set my bag on the tile or in the tub, and breathe. Then I pull back the sheets at the corners, drag my finger along the mattress seam, and look for rust-colored specks or tiny sesame-seed-sized bugs. I peek behind the headboard if it's easy; I scan the bed frame and the piping where fabric meets fabric. No drama, no accusation, just a calm once-over like a pilot checking gauges. If I see anything suspicious, I take a photo and go downstairs with kindness and clarity. Most places will move you immediately. If they can't, I leave and let the receipts and pictures do the arguing later. Your luggage stays off the bed until the room earns the right to hold it. When I check out, I'll quarantine my clothes in a garbage bag if I even suspect an issue, then run a hot wash the moment I can. Paranoia? Maybe. Cheaper than regret? Definitely.

The mid-trip pivot is an art. Sometimes your first pick isn't the right pick, or a better deal appears after you land. You can move without paying twice if you plan the switch like a handoff. I stack checkout and check-in times so I'm never homeless for hours: late checkout at the first place if they'll grant it, early check-in at the second, and luggage storage bridging the gap if neither can help. Hotels will often hold bags for free if you're coming back later that day; rentals can be trickier, but a friendly message to the host solves more problems than you think. I keep a little "transfer kit" on top of my suitcase, chargers, meds, snacks, documents, so the move feels like a walk, not a life event. If the new place is across town, I treat the transfer like a mini field trip and stop somewhere useful on the way: the market near my next kitchen, the laundromat that takes cards, the transit office where I buy the weekly pass.

Sometimes a pivot is about price, sometimes it's about energy. A quiet residential block feels great on day one and lonely on day four. A bargain near nightlife feels exciting until your third 2 a.m. wake-up. It's okay to change the plan. You didn't fail; you learned. What matters is how you negotiate the exit. Be direct and polite: "This isn't the right fit for me. I'm going to check out early. What's the fairest way to handle the unused nights?" With hotels, a same-day checkout is often just the night you used; with rentals, it depends on the cancellation policy and the host's willingness. Clear, early communication buys more grace than a surprise departure ever will.

Every city has oddball beds that don't show up on the first page of searches. University dorms open to travelers in summer. Monasteries and retreat houses rent quiet rooms to anyone willing to follow the house rules. Business-district hotels empty on weekends and will quietly take numbers they'd never publish if you ask. When the usual channels feel stale, walk one block off the tourist drag and look up, signage, doorbells, a chalkboard with a nightly rate. The people who run those places are often standing behind the desk, and people behind desks make deals when you meet them like a neighbor instead of a username.

I budget the way I pack: light, honest, and ready to adapt. For lodging, that means writing the total I'm willing to spend for the whole stay and letting the nights rearrange themselves underneath it. Maybe I splurge the first night to shake off the flight and chase the deal for the next five. Maybe I camp out in a simple extended-stay and drop into the fancy lobby for a coffee when I want the feeling without the bill. The story still writes the same way: sleep where it serves you, not where the algorithm tells you you're supposed to be.

At the end of the day, cheap stays are about asking better questions. Not "What's the nicest hotel I can almost afford?" but "What place lets me wake up rested and ready while leaving me enough to actually do things?" When you frame it like that, the answers multiply. A weekly rate with a kitchen beats three nights of room service. A pet-sitting gig in a neighborhood you've only seen on TV turns into a morning routine that belongs to you. A quick bedbug check buys you peace of mind for free. And a graceful mid-trip pivot—planned like a handoff, not a break-up, keeps your momentum when everyone else is stuck defending a choice they made online at 1 a.m.

That's the system: learn the floor, ask with kindness, check the bed, and stay nimble. If it fits your body, your budget, and your plan, it's the right place, whether it's a capsule for a night or a borrowed set of keys for a month.

Cheap Eats

Food is where most travelers quietly overspend. Not because meals are outrageous, but because hunger makes decisions for you. You land, you're tired, you're excited, and the first menu you see looks like salvation. Cheap eating isn't about skipping flavor or counting napkins. It's about building a small rhythm that keeps you full, flexible, and still curious enough to try the good stuff when it actually appears.

Start with a simple habit the moment you arrive: find the nearest market. Not the souvenir shop masquerading as a market, the real place where local people shop. Buy water or a refillable jug if the tap isn't safe, fruit you can eat with your hands, a loaf of bread, a block of cheese, and something easy like yogurt, nuts, or instant soup. Now breakfast and late-night emergencies are handled without calling room service or stumbling into a tourist trap. If your stay has a kettle or communal kitchen, you've just given yourself options for pennies. I keep a collapsible cup and a tiny packet of seasoning in my bag; paired with a cup of hot water from a café or the hotel lobby, that's a midnight ramen that costs less than a tip.

The second anchor is time. Cities have a rhythm, and prices move with it. Lunch is where great kitchens quietly offer their best value, set menus, weekday deals, portions designed to feed working people. If you build your day around a bigger lunch, you'll spend less than you would on a showy dinner and you'll walk the afternoon happy. Dinner can then be light and local: a bakery sandwich, a skewer from a cart, a bowl of soup from the stand with the longest line. The long line matters. Locals don't wait around for mediocre food. If you're going to gamble, gamble on the place where grandmothers are handing cash to the cashier and the turnover is so fast you can hear the chopping rhythm from the sidewalk.

Walks are a restaurant review you write with your feet. In a ten-minute loop around your lodging you can map breakfast, coffee, and emergency options without opening a single app. Peek at the posted menus, note the openings and closings, and pick one spot that you'll use as your "home" café for the week. When staff see you a second time, life gets easier, extra bread appears, the good table opens up, and sometimes a local tip or neighborhood special comes with your bill. If you want to eat the soul of a place, sit where regulars sit and order what they're eating. Ask the server what people here actually come for. Then say yes.

There's a difference between cheap and stingy. Cheap is smart timing, neighborhood choices, and written limits. Stingy is fear. Don't be afraid to have one real meal each day, the place with counters full of steam and conversation, or the little room with three tables and a handwritten list on the wall. The way you afford that is by keeping your other two meals simple. I often treat breakfast like a pit stop: fruit, yogurt, bread, coffee. By the time lunch hits, I'm ready to sit down somewhere that cooks like someone's aunt is in the kitchen. At night, I keep it light or go hunting for a happy-hour window that lines up before the dinner rush. You're not missing out; you're making room for the moment that's actually worth paying for.

If your lodging includes breakfast, use it with intention. Load your plate with real food, not just pastries that evaporate in an hour. Eggs, beans, vegetables, toast, fuel that carries you through to a late lunch. If breakfast isn't included but there's a fridge, make your own. Markets and bakeries are where the cheapest calories meet the best smell in town. A warm loaf and a jar of spread can anchor three meals for the price of one appetizer in a tourist zone. If you happen to be near a student neighborhood, prices bend to student budgets; that's where you'll find bowls, plates, and combos that are honest about value because the locals demand it.

Street food is a love language, but it still pays to be cautious. Watch for turnover and cleanliness. You want hot food cooked to order or dishes pulled from a pot that's clearly been bubbling all day, not the plate that looks like it's been posing in the sun. Ask what the vendor recommends and start there. If the language is a barrier, point and smile. Money is universal. So is gratitude. When you find a winner, remember it. The second visit is always better than the first because you know what to order and how much to get. Most portions are bigger than you need—share when you can, or ask for half portions and see what happens. Many kitchens will accommodate if you're kind and clear.

Apps can help if you use them like a compass rather than a judge. Reviews will push you to what's famous; walking will push you to what's good. I use apps to check hours, confirm if a place takes cards, and to save a few backups in case my first choice is closed. Groupon-style dining credits can be useful in some cities if the terms are straightforward. Just read the fine print so your "deal" doesn't force you into a three-course set menu you didn't want. If a listing looks too shiny, unlimited drinks, endless tapas—ask yourself why it needs to shout. The best deals let you order exactly what you came for and leave when you're satisfied.

All-inclusive resorts and cruises deserve a special paragraph because they trick you into forgetting the math. The food is "free" once you're on board, but the extras stack quickly. Specialty restaurants, premium coffee, and upcharged snacks are designed to nibble your budget. Eat in the main dining areas first, see if you're still hungry, and save specialty spots for a genuine treat. The buffet is a trap if you stroll in starving; make a small first plate, decide what you really want, and go back once. You'll eat better and feel better, and you won't wander off with a $40 dessert you didn't need because the dining room looked chic.

There's a stealth way to meet your budget without policing every bite: write a daily cap for food and stick it on your notes app. If today is a big lunch day, you'll know dinner is a stroll-and-snack. If you had a thin breakfast, allow yourself the sit-down spot at sunset. The point isn't austerity; it's honesty. You're telling your money where to go instead of wondering where it went. A simple line, "Food cap: $25", is enough to nudge you toward markets, bakeries, and the shaded table where locals take their break.

When in doubt, ask a person who lives there. "If you had ten dollars and wanted to eat well around here, where would you go?" That sentence has led me to stewed meats that fell apart under a spoon, to bowls of noodles I still dream about, and to standing tables where I learned more about a neighborhood in ten minutes than a glossy guide could show me in a week. People like to help. People like to brag about their corner spots. You just have to ask.

Finally, give yourself permission to skip the places built for you. Tourist zones exist to vacuum up time and money. That doesn't make them evil, but it does make them predictable. One avenue over, prices change. Two avenues over, recipes change. The further you drift toward where people live and work, the more honest the menus get. Cheap eats aren't hiding; they're just busy feeding the community that keeps the city running. Join them for a meal, pay in cash when it helps the little guys, and walk back full. That's the win: you spent less, you tasted more, and you learned a city by the way it feeds its own.

Kitchens, Buffets, Gift Cards, and the $10 Food Day

There's a reason I light up when a listing says "kitchenette." A room with a kitchen is a cheat code. It's not about cooking every meal on vacation; it's about the power to make two or three meals a day cost next to nothing. The first stop after check-in is the market: eggs, fruit, greens, bread or tortillas, olive oil, salt, a squeeze-bottle sauce that makes everything taste like you meant it. If there's a freezer, grab a bag of frozen vegetables, cheap, fast, and they don't go bad if you change plans. Cook once, eat twice: a skillet of eggs and peppers in the morning becomes the backbone of a late-night quesadilla or the base for a quick fried rice. You didn't "skip" dinner; you already made it at breakfast.

All-inclusive stays lure you with the sweetest word in travel: included. Many packages cover meals, and some include alcohol, sometimes even the all-you-can-drink kind. That can save real money if you use it with intention. It can also be an upsell trap if you let every specialty coffee, "premium" pour, and late-night snack nibble your budget. Pace yourself. Start in the main dining room or buffet, decide what you actually want, and treat premium venues like a celebration, not a habit. Buffets, whether at resorts or in the city, reward curiosity over hunger. Make a scouting plate, look around for the station the locals are hovering near, and go back once for only the best things. Lunch pricing is usually softer than dinner. That's when the value is hiding in plain sight.

When you're not in an all-inclusive environment, go find your own "all-you-can-eat." Some neighborhoods are full of buffets that charge what regulars can comfortably pay, not what a brochure thinks tourists will tolerate. I treat these like a midday fuel station: one plate built like you mean it, a second for the thing you loved, water to drink, and you're set until the evening walk. Pair that with a market breakfast and a simple, late snack you assemble in your room, and you've quietly turned a spendy food city into a $10–$20 day.

Deals exist; the fine print decides if they help. Restaurant.com can unlock steep discounts if you can work with minimum-spend rules or day-of-week restrictions. Groupon can be great for dining credits, tasting menus, and neighborhood places that want new faces, as long as you screenshot the terms and check whether tax, tip, or alcohol are excluded. If a deal forces you into a rigid three-course set or a fixed time that clashes with your plan, it's not a deal for you. The best offers behave like cash: flexible, clean, and easy to redeem.

Gift cards are another lever. Discount marketplaces like Card-Cash (and, at times, similar sites) sell restaurant and grocery cards below face value. Buy a $50 card for $42, and you've earned an instant 16% off before you even look at a menu. The rules are simple: purchase from a reputable marketplace, redeem quickly, verify the balance the moment it hits your email, and keep your receipt until you've spent every cent. I label the card in my notes, "$50 taco spot, $28.16 remaining", so those little leftovers don't evaporate. If a particular marketplace has spotty reviews in your region, skip it; savings aren't savings if you have to fight for them.

Old-school budgeting still works because it's honest. The envelope system is low-tech and effective: one envelope per day with that day's food money inside. When it's gone, it's gone. If you'd rather go digital, make a daily food cap note on your phone and tick off what you spend as you go. Either way, you're writing the plan, not letting your appetite write it for you. On all-inclusive days, put the cash away completely and focus on memory-making, not menu-scrolling.

Reservations are not the enemy of spontaneity; they're the guardrail that keeps you from "settling" for an expensive, mediocre place because the good one had a ninety-minute wait. OpenTable and similar apps tell you who has space when and sometimes give you points or perks just for booking through them. I use reservations to lock one special meal in a city, usually at lunch when the same kitchen charges less. The rest of the time, I wander, because wandering finds the steam, and steam finds the good food.

Credit cards deserve a grown-up paragraph. Get a card that matches your life, not the internet's. If you rarely dine out at home, a dining-bonus card won't pay you back. If you road trip, a simple cash-back card that hits gas and groceries will do more work than a complicated points card with blackout dates. If a card offers dining credits or statement credits on delivery apps you actually use, great. But the rule stands: rewards never beat interest. Pay it in full or pay cash. Your trip should end with memories, not a monthly bill.

If you want ideas by the dozen, don't sleep on YouTube. Food tour videos are a map of what's good and what's fair. I vibe with channels that walk, pay, and show receipts, no staged clips, just genuine, cheap eats at real counters. Living Bobby is one of those names I recommend when you want to see a city's budget food scene without the hype. Use videos as a shortlist generator: pause, jot down the neighborhoods, and then go see which spots still feel busy and local when you arrive. The internet gives you a head start; your feet finish the race. I love watching YouTube channels like Living Bobby! I remember I watched his "Surviving New York with only $1. It was one of the best, most informative videos I've ever seen, aside from it being truly entertaining. It gave me a different way to approach travel! I wrote down every place he went to, then visited those exact places. It was worth it, from 99-cent pork dumplings in Chinatown to a beautiful market under the Manhattan Bridge.

"See what locals eat" is a principle, not a slogan. Markets tell you what's in season; bakeries tell you what mornings feel like; line-out-the-door lunch counters tell you what workers trust to get them through the afternoon. Ask a cashier what the most-ordered plate is. Ask the person next to you what they'd get if they had five dollars more to spend. People love sharing that knowledge. And if someone tells you about a $1 slice, a $1 taco, a $1 tea egg, or a $1 bowl at a family stall, then go! Those are not just bargains; they're street-level invitations into daily life.

Here's how all of this looks in the wild. You check into a place with a kitchenette. You spend fifteen minutes at the closest market and set yourself up with breakfasts and late-night safety food. You book one reservation for lunch midweek at a restaurant that would have cost you 40% more at dinner. The next day, you use a Restaurant.com certificate at a neighborhood spot with a posted minimum—you ordered exactly enough and tipped well because the servers were moving. Later in the week, you redeem a discounted gift card you bought yesterday for a chain near a museum, and that knocks your cost down again. In between, you walk, you read steam and lines, you say yes to a snack that smells like it was cooked for someone who works around the corner. Your food math disappears into the background, and you're still eating like you wanted to when you dreamed up the trip.

Cheap eats isn't a sacrifice; it's a hospitality choice. You're choosing to meet a city where it lives, to taste what locals can afford, and to leave enough in your pocket for the view at sunset. That's not stingy. That's respect for your budget and for the people who keep the stoves hot.

Snack Kits, Picnics, Coffee Hacks, Drink Math, Reading Menus Like a Local (Now with App Deals & Safety Nets)

Hunger makes people reckless. Planning keeps you generous with yourself and your wallet. The quiet way to win the food budget is to remove the panic purchase. That's what the snack kit is for. Put one together before you leave home or within your first hour in a new city: a handful of nuts, a couple of granola bars, a piece of fruit that travels well, instant soup or noodles, a tiny packet of seasoning, and a collapsible cup. If there's a kettle in your room or a café willing to hand you hot water, you've got a safety meal in five minutes. I've eaten some of my favorite "dinners" sitting on a window ledge with a view, not because the noodles were special, but because they bought me the time to find the place that was.

When the weather cooperates, a picnic is the most honest luxury. There's no dress code, no service fee, and the view is priceless because you picked it. The market is your menu: a warm loaf, a wedge of cheese, olives, tomatoes, something cured or smoked, and a sweet to make the moment stick. Buy napkins and a plastic knife if you need them; they earn their place in the bag by turning a bench into a table. Parks, waterfronts, steps in front of public buildings—all of these become a dining room if you treat the

47

space with respect and clean up after yourself. If there are open-container rules, follow them. The drink can be sparkling water with lime and it will feel festive. You can celebrate without apologizing to your budget later.

Coffee ruins more budgets than steak. It's not the one cappuccino that gets you; it's the fifth, bought in a panic, when you're tired and lost and just want to sit down. I like coffee, but I like choices more. My toolkit is simple: make the first cup where I'm staying, find a bakery with a modestly priced second cup and a seat for ten minutes, and save the fancy shop for an afternoon treat when I actually want to taste something special. If your room has no kettle, cold brew is a traveler's friend. In the evening, stir coffee grounds into a bottle of water, shake, and leave it in the fridge. In the morning, strain it through a paper towel into a cup and add milk or sugar. It won't win awards, but it will keep you from paying six dollars just to sit. Loyalty punch cards, bakery combos, and "coffee included with breakfast" are small edges that add up when you're gone for a week.

The same math runs through everything you drink. Bars sell the seat as much as the beverage. That's not evil just the business model. Decide when you want to pay for the seat, and when you don't. If your plan is a sunset view at a rooftop, fine, own it and enjoy it slowly. If your plan is to meet friends and talk for an hour, consider a market bottle at home-base prices and a picnic before the night begins, then one drink at the bar instead of three. Happy-hour windows exist because restaurants want bodies in seats when it's quiet; learn those hours and you'll taste the same kitchen for less. On cruises and at all-inclusives, pace is a superpower. The alcohol is technically limitless, but your time and sleep are not. Start with water, move to something you love, and let the "unlimited" part be the freedom to say no.

Menus speak a language. If you listen, you'll hear where the value hides. Daily specials usually mean ingredients that are fresh, abundant, or both. Set lunches, workers' menus, and "plates of the day" are designed to feed people who pay attention to price. A board with a few chalked items often points to a kitchen that cooks what it can sell, not what it can photograph. If there's a combo that locals keep ordering, it's two small plates and a drink, a bowl and a bread, a rice and a stew, that's probably the real rhythm of the place. I read the room first, the page second. Are people eating quickly and leaving, or lingering? Are families here? Are workers in uniforms rolling in at noon? Those clues tell me whether I'm in a neighborhood canteen or a showpiece for out-of-towners. Neither is wrong, but one will feed you for less and feel more like the city you came to see.

Tourist districts try to make your choices for you. They lay the photos out like a buffet and make it easy to point at something. But the farther you walk from the main drag, the more the math changes. One street over, prices drop. Two streets over, the menu changes languages and the portions look suspiciously like someone's grandmother is plating them. When I'm unsure, I ask the staff for the dish the regulars order. I don't need a "must-try." I need what keeps the lights on. Nine times out of ten, that's a stew, a grill, a bowl, a pie or something humble, generous, and priced for people who aren't on vacation.

There's a case for being a regular, even for three days. Pick one café, one bakery, and one counter to return to. The second visit is almost always cheaper in some way, maybe with a quiet extra on the plate, maybe with a tip about when to come back for the good soup, maybe because the server remembers you and steers you away from a tourist-priced special that wasn't special at all. In a week, a place can start to feel like yours. That feeling is priceless when you're far from home and trying not to overthink every meal.

Eating cheaply is easier when you admit what actually satisfies you. Maybe that's a generous lunch and a short dinner; maybe it's a morning pastry and a late-night sandwich; maybe it's street food twice and a proper table once. Write it into your day like you write addresses. The budget behaves when the plan exists. If the plan changes, and it will, that's what your snack kit is for. A handful of calories buys you an extra hour to walk, read the neighborhood, and find the room where the good food lives. By the time you sit down, you're choosing instead of settling.

Apps can stack quiet wins if you use them with a little discipline. The big chains run loyalty systems that actually pay you back when you're moving fast and need predictable calories: McDonald's drops free fries and breakfast items after a few visits; Chick-fil-A gives points that turn into entrées; Chipotle awards free sides and bowls if you keep scanning; Starbucks stars convert into drinks and bakery items and sometimes bump you into promos you'd never see otherwise. The trick is to treat these apps like a toolbox, not a diet. Load gift cards when there's a bonus, order ahead when it saves you money or time, and grab the freebie when it appears—but don't chase points with purchases you wouldn't have made. If a city is expensive, rolling one chain meal into your week can stabilize the budget so you can say yes to the local place that matters tomorrow.

There's also no shame in packing a lunch. If times are tight, a sandwich in a zip bag, a piece of fruit, and a bottle of water will carry you through a museum day without the café bill. Hotels often have ice machines and hot water; between those and your snack kit, you can eat simply for a day and put that money toward an experience you'll remember. Ramen noodles are the undefeated travel equalizer. With a kettle or a cup of hot water, you've got something warm, salty, and enough to reset your mood while you hunt down a better option for dinner.

If you're traveling within the United States and you qualify, SNAP (food stamps) is a legal, valid way to keep groceries affordable on the road. It's meant for food you prepare yourself, not hot prepared meals, and rules vary by state and by retailer. Some areas also participate in farmers' market matches that double part of your spend for fresh produce. If you're in real need, don't wait: local food banks and community fridges can bridge a hard week. Libraries, houses of worship, and the 2-1-1 hotline can point you to nearby options with dignity and speed. None of this is a step backward. It's a step toward taking care of yourself so you can keep moving forward.

YouTube can help if you use it with a filter. Look for creators who walk, pay, and eat like you would. I learn more from a shaky phone video of a busy lunch counter than from a glossy montage that never shows a receipt. Channels that share neighborhoods, exact prices, and public transit directions are worth their weight in meals. Use them to sketch a neighborhood list, then let your senses finish the job: steam, sounds, and the kind of line that forms when people eat there because it's Tuesday, not because it's famous.

If there's one habit that keeps cheap eats joyful, it's kindness. Be gracious if you get the last seat. Buy bottled water from the same kiosk twice. Tip as generously as your budget allows in places where it's customary, and round up when it isn't. Small generosity has a way of coming back as extra bread, an extra minute at the table, a suggested dish off the menu that ends up being the memory you talk about later. Money matters. People matter more. When both are respected, you'll leave full, and you'll leave the city a tiny bit better than you found it.

Cheap Cruises

Never feel guilty about traveling. Cruises are one of the most misunderstood parts of budget travel. Some people see them as floating hotels that are too expensive, others think they're only for retirees, and plenty of travelers assume the hidden fees will ruin their budget. The truth? A cruise can either be the cheapest, easiest way to see multiple destinations or one of the most frustrating money drains you'll ever book.

The difference lies in the line you choose, the timing, and how you play the onboard game. To show both sides of the coin, I'm including two personal stories: one where a cruise line gave me unforgettable value, and another where it failed me in every possible way.

Why I Love Carnival Cruise Lines

I'm sure other ships offer more amenities, but Carnival Cruise Lines has a special place in my heart. I love the kind, friendly environment as well as the luxury style dining. I grew up on

Carnival. They, for the most part, were affordable. In fact, they're even more affordable in the present day of 2025 than they were back in 2005. If you go on their website, you get deals as far as the eye can see. I recommend taking full advantage of them as well. Carnival Cruise Lines is a place not just for families to enjoy, but also for single people. Finding a few friends on the ship and experiencing new people has never been easier. With dining options that will blow your mind, full breakfast bar, lunch bar, dinner buffet, and midnight snacks, you'll truly be left wanting more. I also have to mention their fine dining options and the captain's ball, making you feel as though you're reliving the 1930s with their beautiful decorative themes and dinner with a show. Speaking of a show, you're never far from some form of entertainment among the big ships with either clapping or laughter at every corner. You won't have to search long for the oohs and aahs of happy, inter-intrigued people. Might I recommend the All-You-Can-Drink Alcohol Pass? Truly worth the money, I assure you. And if you're a fan of upside-down pineapples, make it known and it'll be known if you know you know!

Carnival represents the best of what cruising can be: affordable, social, entertaining, and full of value at every corner. It proves that with the right cruise line, you don't have to sacrifice comfort or fun to travel cheap.

My Disappointing Experience on MSC Meraviglia (March 30 to April 6)

Cruising is supposed to be a chance to relax, explore new destinations, and create memories that stick with you for life.

When I booked my first trip with MSC Cruises aboard the MSC Meraviglia, sailing March 30 to April 6, I expected exactly that. Instead, what I got was a frustrating week full of delays, misleading excursions, broken promises, and dismissive service that left me feeling like I wasted both my time and money.

The first sign of trouble came with our stop in Florida. According to the itinerary, we were scheduled to dock at 1 PM. That should have given me a full afternoon to spend time with family and enjoy the plans I had already arranged.

Instead, we did not dock until after 5 PM, and by 9 PM, we were already pulling away again. That gave me less than four hours, not even half of what I was promised. Because of this delay, I missed time with my family and lost money on non-refundable reservations.

The excuse given was the weather. But standing on deck, many passengers, myself included, noticed the ship shaking and crawling unusually slow. It felt more like a mechanical issue that nobody wanted to admit.

The next major disappointment came in the Bahamas. I paid for an island tour, expecting to explore cultural sites, hear local history, and visit landmarks like Atlantis.

What I got was completely different. I was crammed into a small van with other passengers and driven from one gift shop to another, each stop clearly arranged to funnel us into spending money.

The worst part came when we were told we had arrived at Atlantis. Instead of the world-famous resort, we were dropped in an empty parking lot with nothing but a Wendy's and a Subway. We were given 25 minutes to look around, even though the real Atlantis property was nowhere in sight.

On the drive, we passed important sites like the U.S. Embassy, yet the driver gave no commentary at all. No history, no culture, no explanations. Just silence except for the drivers laughing and chatting among themselves while we sat in the back, confused.

This was not an island tour. It was a scam, plain and simple.

The part of this cruise I was most excited for, the highlight that made me book MSC in the first place, was their private island, Ocean Cay.

Ocean Cay was supposed to be the crown jewel of the trip. Instead, we never went. Once again, the excuse was weather, but the reality told a different story. I stood outside, looked up, and saw calm seas and clear skies. Passengers looked at each other in disbelief, wondering how such perfect conditions could cancel a stop.

It did not just feel like a letdown. It felt dishonest.

What turned this trip from disappointing to infuriating was how staff responded when passengers voiced concerns. Instead of empathy, we got dismissal. Instead of answers, we got shrugs.

In one instance, when I pressed an issue, a crew member

outright told me, That is not our problem. That moment summed up the entire tone of the cruise.

Cruising is not just about the itinerary, it is about service, energy, and making passengers feel valued. On MSC, I felt like an inconvenience.

When I reflect on this trip, the truth is painful. Out of seven days, I only truly enjoyed one day on land. The rest was wasted on delays, excuses, and cancellations.

I vlogged the entire trip, producing a three part video series and a seven minute clip specifically showing how staff dismissed concerns. These will be posted on my social channels to help future travelers make an informed choice before booking MSC.

This was my first experience with MSC Cruises, and it will also be my last. The Meraviglia may look beautiful from the outside, but behind the shiny lobby and polished photos lies poor organization, misleading excursions, broken promises, and customer service that fails when it matters most.

Cruises are supposed to create memories worth keeping. The only memories I am left with from this trip are the things I missed, the money I lost, and the way I was treated when I tried to speak up.

For anyone considering MSC, learn from my mistake. If you value your time, money, and experience, book elsewhere.

Lessons from Both Stories

Carnival proves how cheap cruising can work: affordable fares, great food, constant entertainment, and an environment where you feel welcomed. MSC, on the other hand, shows how quickly things can unravel: misleading excursions, wasted time, dismissive staff, and a company more focused on excuses than passenger experience.

Both experiences are valuable. One reminds you to look for cruise lines with a proven track record of customer satisfaction. The other is a warning to research carefully before booking, read reviews, and understand that not all "deals" are worth it.

Booking Strategies & Timing

A cruise can either be the best deal of your life or the fastest way to blow a hole in your budget. The difference usually comes down to when you book, where you sail, and how flexible you are.

Book Early or Book Late

The golden rule with cruises: either book way ahead or way last-minute. Middle ground is where you overpay.

- Early Bird: If you want a specific ship, route, or cabin type (like balconies or suites), book as soon as itineraries drop. Prices are lowest then, and you get first pick of rooms.
- Last-Minute: If you live near a port, last-minute deals can be insane. Cruise lines would rather fill cabins cheap than sail empty. You'll need flexibility and no expensive flights to the port, but the savings can be hundreds per person.

Off-Season is King

Peak summer and holiday cruises will wreck your budget. The cheapest windows are:

- September – October: Kids are back in school, summer rush is over, hurricane season scares off some travelers, and prices tank.
- Early December: Before Christmas, fares plummet. You'll sail cheap while ships decorate for the holidays.
- May & September in Alaska: Shoulder season cuts prices almost in half compared to July.
- Spring & Fall in the Mediterranean: Avoid summer crowds and pay far less.

Repositioning Cruises: The Hidden Gem

Repositioning cruises are when ships move from one region to another, like Europe to the Caribbean in the fall, or the Caribbean back to Europe in spring. Because these itineraries are one-way and heavy on sea days, they're often ignored. Which is crazy, because they can be the cheapest cruises in the world. Two weeks across the Atlantic with meals, entertainment, and lodging included can cost less than a one-way flight.

Use Deal Alerts and Aggregators

Don't waste time checking 20 sites daily. Let the deals come to you. Subscribe to:

- VacationsToGo.com – a leader in last-minute deals.
- CruiseCritic Deals Section – reviews plus discounts.
- Going.com (Scott's Cheap Flights) – not just for flights; they highlight cruise bundles too.
- Ship loyalty emails – Carnival and Norwegian send out constant promo codes and "48-hour sale" alerts.

Watch Out for Fake "Discounts"

Cruise lines love to advertise "40% off" or "BOGO deals." Here's the truth: they raise the base fare, then apply the "discount." Always compare the total after taxes, fees, and gratuities. The only real discount is the one that lowers your final payment.

Hidden Costs, Real Deals & How to Beat Them

One of the reasons cruises get a bad reputation is because of the "hidden" costs. The fare looks cheap, but once you're onboard, you're hit with drink charges, excursion markups, gratuities, Wi-Fi, specialty dining, and a dozen little extras. If you're not ready, those small bites add up and turn your budget-friendly trip into an expensive one.

But here's the flip side: if you know how to dodge the traps and grab the right deals, you can cruise for less than it costs to stay home.

The Groupon Factor

Most people don't even think to check Groupon for cruises, but it's one of the easiest hacks in the book. Groupon on often lists deeply discounted packages, especially for Caribbean, Bahamas, and Mexico sailings. These are usually unsold cabins that cruise lines want to unload quickly. If you're flexible with dates and don't mind grabbing what's available, you can score prices that shock most travelers.

"The key to make your money last is by writing it down." If you track your budget and write out exactly what you're willing to spend, you'll start noticing just how cheap some Groupon cruise listings really are. It's all about being intentional.

Pro tip: Groupon cruises often come bundled with extras like drink credits or onboard cash. Always read the fine print, but don't sleep on it, some of the best cruise steals hide there.

Carnival's Thank-You Discounts

Another secret deal comes straight from Carnival themselves. Once you sail with them, they send you a thank-you email after your trip. Hidden in that email is often an exclusive offer for another sailing, sometimes a full 7-day cruise for $300–$400.

That's not a typo. Carnival would rather reward loyal travelers than market endlessly to new ones. These post-cruise deals are pure gold, but you have to act quickly and accept the fact that you can't always choose the exact ship or route.

Cruise Deals Rule #1: Don't be picky.

Be open to location, dates, and even ship class. If you're flexible, you'll catch the lifetime deals that everyone else misses.

- Shore days: Don't book cruise excursions through the line, DIY them for less; use skip-the-line where it meaningfully saves time.
- Drinks math: If not on an all-inclusive/bev package, BYO within policy and price out packages vs à la carte.
- Museums/attractions on port days: Buy tickets ahead, many museums are free—plan port time, not queues.

Hidden Costs to Watch For (and Beat)

- Gratuities: Usually $14–$20 per day, per person. Budget for it, it's non-negotiable.
- Drinks: Alcohol packages can hit $60+ per day. If you don't drink much, skip it and stick to free tea, coffee, and water.
- Excursions: Ship tours are overpriced. Book through locals or use apps like Viator to save half.
- Wi-Fi: Almost never worth it. Disconnect and use free Wi-Fi in port cafés instead.
- Specialty Dining: Buffets and main dining are included and usually more than enough. Treat specialty restaurants as optional splurges, not mandatory costs.

Port Hacks, Onboard Tricks & Where to Find Deals

A cruise fare gets you the room, the meals, and the shows, but the real test of your budget comes when you step off the ship. Ports are where cruise lines make their money. They sell overpriced excursions, funnel you through duty-free shops, and nudge you toward activities that burn cash. If you're smart, you can dodge all that and still have a better time.

DIY Excursions

The number one rule of port days: you don't have to buy the ship's excursion. Cruise-arranged tours often cost double what the same experience costs locally.

- In Nassau, you can grab a $5 taxi to the beach instead of paying $60 for a "Beach Day Package."
- In Cozumel, renting a scooter and exploring on your own is way cheaper (and more fun) than a guided bus ride.
- In Grand Turk, the beach is literally right off the dock, no need to pay anyone a dime.

Check TripAdvisor, Viator, or even Facebook groups for your sailing before you go. You'll find other passengers planning independent tours you can join at half the price.

Free or Cheap Port Days

Some of the best port activities are completely free. Wandering old towns, hitting public beaches, hiking nearby trails, or just soaking up local culture doesn't cost a thing. Not every port needs to be a shopping spree.

Pro tip: Bring your own snorkel gear or water shoes from home. Renting at port racks up fast.

Onboard Tricks

Your savings don't stop when you're back on the ship.

- Bring Your Own Snacks: Pack trail mix, protein bars, or chips for port days. Buying snacks onboard or at the dock will double your costs.
- Cabin Upgrades: If the ship isn't full, you can sometimes get a cheap upgrade at the service desk. Always ask politely, the worst they can say is no.
- Loyalty Programs: Sign up even if it's your first cruise. Carnival, Royal Caribbean, and Norwegian all offer small perks (free drinks, priority boarding, cabin discounts) for repeat travelers.

Where to Find Cruise Deals

Websites can make or break your budget. Don't just book through the cruise line's official page, compare across platforms.

- VacationstoGo.com – One of the best-kept secrets in cruising. Their "90-Day Ticker" lists last-minute cruise discounts worldwide. You can find 7-day cruises for under $400 if you're quick.
- Groupon – Perfect for unsold Caribbean and Bahamas itineraries. You'll often get bonus perks like onboard credit.
- CruiseCritic.com – Reviews plus a deals section that catches short-lived sales.
- Going.com (Scott's Cheap Flights) – Better known for airfare, but they also send out bundle alerts that include cruise packages.
- Loyalty emails – Once you've cruised once, never ignore the thank-you emails. Carnival, Norwegian, and Royal Caribbean all quietly slip in exclusive codes.

The trick isn't to obsessively refresh websites every day. It's to put yourself on the right lists, set price alerts, and be flexible. Remember, you're not chasing a specific ship, you're chasing value.

Cruise Myths vs. Cruise Reality

People love to talk trash about cruises. If you've never been on one, you've probably heard the same lines: "Cruises are too expensive," "The food sucks," "You'll get seasick," "It's just for old people." Most of the time, these myths are either outdated or exaggerated. Let's clear the air.

Myth #1: Cruises are too expensive.

Reality: A cruise can be cheaper than staying home. Think about it, your fare covers lodging, meals, entertainment, and transportation between countries. If you tried to book a hotel + 3 meals a day + nightly shows + plane rides between each destination, you'd pay triple. Carnival often runs 7-night cruises for $400 or less. That's less than $60 a day, all-in.

Myth #2: Cruises are only for old people.

Reality: Maybe 30 years ago. Today's cruises target every demographic. Carnival is loud, fun, and family-friendly. Norwegian and Royal Caribbean have water parks, zip lines, and nightclubs. Even Disney caters to families with kids. The crowd depends on the line and season; you can find anything from college spring breakers to retirees on the same ship.

Myth #3: The food is bad.

Reality: Cruise food has levels. The buffets can be hit-or-miss, but main dining rooms often feel like fine dining, steaks, seafood, and plated desserts are standard. Carnival's "midnight pizza" is legendary, and Royal Caribbean has full-on steakhouse options included. If you want to splurge, specialty restaurants can rival land-based restaurants, but you don't need them to eat well.

Myth #4: You'll get seasick.

Reality: Modern ships are massive and stabilized. Unless you're sailing in hurricane season or you're very prone to motion sickness, you'll barely notice movement. Bring Dramamine just in case, but most first-timers are surprised by how smooth the ride feels.

Myth #5: You'll feel trapped.

Reality: On a 3,000-passenger ship, "trapped" is the last word that comes to mind. Pools, gyms, spas, casinos, theaters, comedy club, there's too much to do. And at port, you're off the ship exploring new countries. If you feel trapped, it's because you didn't go looking for fun.

Myth #6: Cruises nickel-and-dime you.

Reality: This one is half-true. Cruise lines will try to sell you drink packages, excursions, Wi-Fi, and specialty dining. But here's the hack: you don't need any of it. If you stick to included meals, free entertainment, and DIY port days, you can cruise dirt cheap. The upsells are optional, not mandatory.

Cruises are like any other form of travel: they're what you make them. If you plan badly, don't do your research, and buy every add-on, you'll walk away broke and bitter. If you go in with a budget, track your spending, and stay flexible on dates and destinations, you'll walk away with one of the best travel bargains on the planet.

Carnival showed me how fun, cheap, and memorable cruising can be. MSC reminded me why research and timing matter. Between the two, I learned the ultimate lesson: cruises aren't risky if you play the game, they're rewarding.

Bottom line: cruises aren't the enemy, careless booking is. Pick the right line, sail in the right window, ignore the upsells you don't need, and a week at sea can cost less than a week at home. Carnival showed me the ceiling on value when service, food, and energy match the price; MSC showed me the floor when excuses replace honesty. Use both lessons. Book early or last-minute, chase shoulder seasons, DIY your shore days, pay in local currency, and keep screenshots like they're gold. Do that and a cruise stops being a gamble and starts being your cheapest multi-country trip with beds, meals, and memories already built in.

Cheap Transportation

Move Like A Local: Cheap Transportation That Doesn't Suck. Getting there is half the cost, and sometimes half the stress. Cheap transportation is not about suffering through 12-hour rides or walking everywhere. It is about choosing the right ride for the right distance, then stacking tiny advantages, flexible timing, local passes, and a few scripts that protect your wallet. Use this as your starter pack, then tweak it for the city you are in.

The 80/20 Of Getting Around

- Within the city: walk first, public transit second, rideshare last. Every city has its own rhythm, but this order saves the most money without killing your fun.
- City to city, short to medium range: buses beat trains on price, trains beat buses on comfort and reliability. Fly only when distance or time makes ground travel silly.
- Overnight moves: if a bus or train is safe and reasonably direct, sleep through the travel and wake up in the new city, no extra hotel night.

Public Transit Like A Local, Without Getting Lost

- Day or weekly passes: many cities offer unlimited ride passes that pay for themselves in 3 to 4 trips. If you will take more than that, buy the pass and stop thinking about it.
- Contactless caps: some systems cap your daily or weekly spend when you tap with the same card or phone. After you hit the cap, rides are effectively free. Ask a station agent or check the official transit site.
- Airport rail or bus: before you default to rideshare, price the airport train or express bus. Often it is 70 to 90 percent cheaper and just as fast during rush hour.
- Transfers and timing: when in doubt, ride the line that runs most frequently, even if it is not the perfect route. High frequency means fewer chances to get stuck waiting.
- Map confidence trick: screenshot the transit map and mark your station with a star. If your signal drops, you still know where you are and where you are getting off.
- Mode pivots: prioritize trains and buses over short haul flights when they are cheaper.
- DIY tours vs markups: check paid tours to see their routes, then run the same sights yourself for less.

Money On The Move

- ATM and FX: withdraw once to cut fees, get local cash on arrival, at card terminals choose local currency and decline dynamic currency conversion.

Rideshare And Taxis Without The Surge Penalty

- Walk one block: prices can drop 10 to 30 percent if you

request pickup away from stadiums, arenas, or airport arrival lanes.

- Time your ride: leave 10 to 15 minutes before or after the mass let out. If your app supports price alerts, wait for the dip.
- Fixed fare script, taxis: "Meter or fixed? What is the total to [destination], including tolls? If it is $[fair price], we are good." Carry small bills. Be ready to say thanks and wave for the next car.
- Shared rides: if safety and timing check out, shared options cut costs, especially to and from airports.
- Avoid airport premium zones: some airports allow pickups in economy lots with a free shuttle. That 8 minute ride can cut your fare in half.

Buses, The Cheapest Intercity Workhorse

- When buses win: under 6 hours, last minute travel, or you are starting or ending in smaller cities. Prices can be shockingly low.
- Overnight strategy: choose departures around 10 to 11 pm, wear layers, pack earplugs and an eye mask, sit mid coach. Now your ticket is also your hotel.
- Station savvy: major hubs can be chaotic. Keep valuables on you, arrive 20 to 30 minutes early to board calmly and pick your seat.
- Snacks and water: stations overprice everything. Bring your own and avoid paying $7 for water.

Trains, Pay For Reliability, Still Save

- When trains win: busy corridors, winter weather, or places where rail is the backbone. Trains leave on time more often and arrive downtown.
- Savings moves: book early bird fares, ride off peak, consider regional trains over premium expresses. A 20 minute longer ride can be half the price.
- Seat strategy: if seat selection is free, pick forward facing near the middle carriages for a smoother ride and quicker exits.

Rental Cars The Right Way, Or Not At All

- When to rent: rural trips, national parks, multi stop itineraries, or when 3 to 4 people split the cost. Otherwise, it is usually cheaper to combine transit with occasional rideshare.
- Off airport pickup: airport locations bake in fees. Compare the same company a few miles away, sometimes it is $15 to $30 per day less. A short rideshare to the branch can still put you ahead.
- Fuel and toll traps: decline pre paid fuel unless you will return on fumes. Ask exactly how tolls work. Some companies auto enroll you in expensive programs.
- Photo everything: take walk around photos at pickup and drop off, tires, windshield, roof, interior. Keep them 60 to 90 days in case someone invents a scratch later.
- Insurance sanity: if your personal policy or credit card covers rentals, bring proof and decline the extras. If you do not have coverage, budget for the basic plan so one fender bender does not nuke your savings.
- One way math: one ways can be worth it when time is more

valuable than money. Compare the drop fee to the cost of backtracking.

Micro Mobility And Walking, The Underestimated Win

- Bikes and scooters: for distances under two miles, shared bikes or scooters beat cars in dense cores and cost a fraction of a taxi.
- Walk the first or last mile: a 10 to 15 minute walk often replaces a transfer or a surge ride, and you will see real neighborhoods, not just main streets.
- Safety check: wear a helmet if possible, use lights at night, stick to marked lanes or slow streets. If it feels sketchy, hop off and walk.

The Free First Day Plan, Transport Edition

1. Pick a free anchor in a different part of town, market, park, waterfront.
2. Walk if it is under 30 minutes, otherwise take the highest frequency bus or train.
3. Add one paid highlight max, a museum ticket, a viewpoint, a rental bike hour.
4. Ride back after the crowds. If surge is wild, sit for 20 minutes or walk one stop away.

Scripts You Will Actually Use

- Transit window help: "Hi, what is the fastest route from here to [place] right now, bus or train? Is there a day pass that caps my fare?"

- Rideshare surge bail out: "That price is high. I will walk to [nearby street] and check again."
- Rental desk armor: "I am declining additional insurance and fuel packages. Please keep the base rate as booked."
- Taxi price lock: "$[fair total] including tolls? Great, I have exact cash."

Pre Trip Transport Checklist

- Airport train or bus price vs rideshare, each way.
- Day or weekly pass cost vs pay per ride math.
- Nearby airports for cheaper flights, drive to cruise ports.
- Bus vs train times and prices, overnight options safe.
- Rental car: off airport quote, insurance plan, toll policy, photo checklist.
- Screenshots of routes, maps, and booking confirmations saved offline.

Local Wheels And Workarounds, Uber, Parking, Turo, U Haul, Walking, Mopeds, Boats

Transportation is not just a cost line, it is an experience. The car you choose, or do not choose, can drop you inside a neighborhood you would never see from a tour bus. Use taxis, Ubers, rentals, local transit, and even oddball options to stretch your budget and expand your story.

Uber, Taxis, And Local Rides, Quick Wins

- Uber is fast, usually cheaper than taxis in busy cores, and shows the fare before you move. Use it as the backup, not the default. Walk or take transit first.

- Taxi script, lock the price: "Meter or fixed? What is the total to [destination], including tolls? If it is $[fair price], we are good." Bring small bills. Be ready to walk if the number is not right.
- Airport trick: some airports let you request pickup from an economy lot with a free shuttle. That 8 minute detour can cut your fare in half.
- Local apps: in many countries, local rideshare apps beat Uber on price and coverage. Ask staff or your host which app locals actually use.

Parking Without The Pain

- Use parking apps, ParkMobile, SpotHero, ParkWhiz, or the city's official app. Book a garage near your activities and compare in by or out by rules. Pre booking often saves 30 to 60 percent over drive up rates.
- Neighborhood swap: park in a cheaper district near a frequent transit line and ride in. Ten minutes on a train beats $40 per day downtown.
- Street rules snapshot: screenshot the block's signage, sweep days, permit zones, meter hours, so you do not forget what you agreed to.

Peer To Peer Car Rentals

- Turo, often misheard as Toro: hosts often undercut big agencies, especially for one day hops and off airport pickups. Pros are self service pickup, wide vehicle range, less hard sell. Watch mileage caps, cleaning rules, and insurance choices.

- Approval ease: license and app profile do the heavy lifting. Keep pickup and return photos, time stamped, in case of claims.

The Extreme Saver Hack, Cargo Pickups And Box Trucks

- U Haul in town rates exist, but add mileage, fuel, taxes, and optional coverage. For very short distances and daytime use, it can beat a standard rental. For long mileage, it will not.
- Hardware store pickups often rent by the hour. Great for a half day run to beaches, trailheads, or markets. Return rules are strict.
- Reality check: seats are limited, rides are basic, and some companies do not intend these vehicles for casual passenger use. Verify insurance, seating, and local rules first. If it passes the test and the math wins, it is a legit money move.

Walk It, See More

- Plan a 30 minute walking radius around a free anchor, park, market, waterfront. You will spend less and discover more.
- First or last mile rule: walk one stop away from the busiest area before calling a ride. Prices drop, stress drops, and you will probably spot a snack you actually want.

Mopeds, Motorcycles, And Two Wheels

- In beach towns and smaller cities, renting a moped can be the lowest cost, highest freedom move.
- Safety and legality: helmets always. Check license requirements and insurance before you pay. Some places require

an International Driving Permit for engines.
- Rain plan: if the sky looks iffy, have a bus or train backup.
- Deposit photos: take time stamped photos of every angle at pickup and return.

Trains, Trams, And The Local Local Way

- Take trains when the country runs on rail. Regional trains are cheaper than premium expresses and put you in city centers.
- Trams and minibuses, colectivos, daladalas, jeepneys, marshrutkas, names vary, are how locals move. They are cheap and frequent. Ask where to stand and what to pay.

Small Airports, Puddle Jumpers, And Water

- Regional hops can beat a 6 hour bus. Luggage limits are tight. Book early and travel light.
- Boats and water taxis, ferries, long tails, pangas, often give you the cheapest scenic route. Confirm the last boat back to avoid paying for a private ride.
- Animals as transport: if you choose to ride, pick reputable operators who treat animals well. Or opt for a photo and support with a tip.

Ask Locals, Use Travel Blogs As A Compass

- Ask, "If you were me and wanted to spend almost nothing, how would you get to [spot]?" People love giving the answer no app shows.
- Blogs and YouTube are idea machines, then verify hours and

prices on official sites because last mile details change.

Quick Math To Keep You Honest

- Parking vs transit: if garage and meters will run $30 per day but a 7 day transit pass is $25, park once and ride all week.
- Turo vs agency: Turo at $42 per day plus $12 insurance vs agency $58 per day plus add ons. After taxes, parking, and mileage caps, which is really cheaper. Write the all in on paper.
- U Haul headline rate: $19.95 plus miles times rate plus fuel plus taxes plus coverage. If you cannot keep miles low, it is not the bargain you want.

More Scripts Worth Saving

- Parking app chat: "Does this garage honor advance rates on late exit. Any grace period if I am 15 minutes over."
- Turo message: "Hi. Can you confirm daily mileage and pickup details. I will upload pickup and return photos. Any flexibility on return time."
- Scooter desk: "Is an IDP required here. Helmet included. I will take photos before and after."
- Boat kiosk: "When is the last shared boat back tonight. What is the price if I miss it and need a private ride."

The Daily Play That Keeps Costs Down And Fun Up

Start each day with a free anchor in a new area. Walk the first mile. Use transit for the long leg. Rideshare the last half mile only if your feet or the clock demand it. If you need wheels, compare Turo vs agency vs cargo pickup on an all in basis. Ask a local how they would do it for cheap, then do that. Transportation done right becomes part of the memory, the tram through the market, the water taxi at sunset, the scooter along the beach road. Spend less moving and you will have more for the moments.

Intercity Strategy, Night Moves, Safety, And Transfers

Cheap transportation is not about one mode forever. It is about pivoting. Bus when you are price sensitive and flexible, train when reliability matters, rideshare or rental when time is the limit, walking or bikes for the last mile. Use these for city to city moves, late night logistics, safety, rail passes, carpools, and airport transfers.

Intercity Game Plan, Pick The Right Tool For The Distance

- 0 to 2 hours, regional hops: buses or regional trains. Choose the downtown to downtown fastest. If times are similar, bus wins on price, train on comfort.
- 2 to 6 hours, the sweet spot: buses quietly dominate on price. Trains can win for on time arrivals and laptop friendly space.
- 6 to 10 hours: compare overnight bus or train vs a budget flight. If you can sleep and the route is safe, overnight saves a hotel night. If not, an early flight may be cheaper after you price the cost of lost sleep.
- 10 plus hours: fly unless the rail line is scenic, fast, and fairly priced. Long overland rides are memorable but can tax your energy.

Rule of thumb: if you leave and arrive in the city core, and your door to door time beats flying by 90 minutes or less, rail usually wins. If prices are far apart and your schedule is flexible, bus wins.

Night Moves, Arrive Rested Instead Of Wrecked

- Seat selection: center of the bus or train, forward facing, away from doors and restrooms to reduce noise and foot traffic.
- Comfort kit: hoodie, light scarf, earplugs or eye mask, water, snacks, portable battery. A $10 neck pillow pays for itself tomorrow.
- Split routes smartly: if no direct overnight exists, take a late evening hop to a mid point, short sleep near the station, dawn departure.
- Daylight arrivals: easier to navigate, buy a SIM, and sort passes when staff are working.

Safety Plays You Will Actually Use

- Bag strategy: one small backpack under your feet with passport, phone, money. One small carry on overhead. Nothing valuable in the hold.
- Platform awareness: arrive a little early, keep earbuds low, stand where there are people. If it feels off, move closer to staff or bright areas.
- Night arrivals: screenshot walking directions and a backup taxi stand or rideshare pickup point. If your gut says taxi, taxi. Money saved is not worth feeling unsafe.
- Seat neighbor check: if someone's energy is off, change cars

or seats at the next stop. No explanation needed.
- Paper backup: offline tickets, PDFs, and one written address. Phones die at the worst time.

Carpools And Ride Shares, The In Between That Saves

- When to consider: underserved corridors, last minute weekends, or medium hops where drivers are already going your way.
- How to pick: verified drivers with consistent reviews. Read car rules, bags, music, pets, quiet.
- Cost and comfort math: prices can drop to bus level with car comfort, but times are less fixed. Keep a backup bus or train if a ride cancels.
- Meet point: choose busy, well lit pickups near stations or cafes. Share the ride details with a friend.

Rail Passes, Make Them Work For You

- Passes win when you have 3 to 7 substantial train days within a month, or back to back travel days where rail dominates.
- Single tickets win if you only have one or two long rides, or cities tied together by cheap buses or short flights.
- Reservations: some passes require seat reservations with small fees. Add that to the math.
- Itinerary trick: build burst days, train heavy, and base days, stay put, instead of lots of tiny hops.

Long Distance Buses, How To Not Hate Them

- Choose frequency and reputation. Hourly runs and clean

equipment beat rock bottom fares that strand you if one bus fails.

- Rest stops: ask the driver how long. Set a timer. Missing a re board is the costliest $2 snack you will ever buy.
- Two seat tactic: on unassigned coaches, boarding early increases your chance to spread out on light departures. Be considerate if the coach fills.
- Weather buffer: in winter, pick earlier departures because delays stack later.

Airport To City Transfers, Do Not Burn Your Savings At The Finish Line

- Price rail or bus first. They often cost a fraction of rideshares and can be faster in rush hour.
- Luggage reality: heavy bags or kids may make the second cheapest option the smartest option.
- Group math: 3 to 4 people can make a taxi or Uber cheaper per person than the express train. Do the division.
- Late night arrivals: if rail shuts down early, check night buses or official shared shuttles. Screenshot stop locations before you fly.
- Cheap pickups: some airports allow rideshare pickup in economy lots. Shuttle there and request to dodge terminal surcharges.

Luggage And Packing To Move Faster, And Cheaper

- Personal item only beats fees and stairs.
- Compression cubes keep you sorted and small.
- Water and snack kit saves you from overpriced cafe cars.

- Layer for temperature swings. One light rain shell beats three emergency sweaters.

Accessibility And Comfort Without Overspending

- If $10 to $20 more gets you a real seat assignment or extra legroom on a long ride, buy your future self the upgrade.
- Check elevator status and assistance options. Many services pre board travelers who need extra time.

Edge Cases Worth Knowing

- Border crossings: overland routes may check passports on board or at stations. Keep documents handy.
- Festival weeks: demand spikes. Book earlier or base in a nearby city and commute in.
- Holiday timetables: Sunday and holiday schedules run less frequently. Do not assume weekday headways.

Station, Airport, And Carpool Scripts

- Station help: "Is there a day or weekly pass that caps my fare. Which line runs most frequently to [area] right now."
- Overnight seat ask: "Any open rows toward the middle of the coach. I am hoping to sleep safely and will move if it fills."
- Airport desk: "Is the express bus faster than the train at this hour. Where does it drop off downtown."
- Carpool confirm: "Hi. Confirming pickup spot, a buffer on ETA, and space for one small bag. If anything changes I will take the 7:20 bus as backup."

The Big Move Checklist Before You Book

- Compare bus vs train vs flight door to door time and total cost, all fees.
- Identify one overnight option and decide if your body can handle it this trip.
- Pick a safety first arrival time if possible, daylight beats late night.
- Screenshot tickets, routes, backup stops, and offline maps.
- Share your itinerary with a friend, set a check in message for arrival.

Getting Around Without Getting Got

Everybody loves bragging about a $200 flight. After you land is where budgets quietly die. Think like a local, not a tourist. Public transit is your best friend. Before you arrive, search "public transport card [city name]." Day or week passes often pay for themselves in two rides. Apps like Citymapper, Moovit, and Rome2Rio show buses, subways, ferries, and trains in real time, a GPS for your wallet. In many cities, a $5 metro card takes you further than a $50 Uber.

In smaller places or islands, look for shared rides, colectivos, songthaews, tuk tuks, moto taxis. They move like community buses. Hop in, pay the local price, keep it moving. In Europe, night buses and overnight trains are a cheat code. You sleep and travel at the same time, one less hotel bill, one more story.

If you need a car, check Turo, Getaround, or local groups before a counter. If you only need wheels for hours, car sharing beats traditional rental. Record a quick video before you drive off. Photos and proof protect your peace. And do not bleed cash in airport taxis. Never ride without checking the meter or a fixed price. Apps like Bolt, Grab, and InDriver exist in many countries, safer and cheaper with fewer wrong turn surprises.

Long term, walk and wander. Every step saves money, burns calories, and shows you things you will never see from a window. Some of the best travel stories start with "I got lost and found this little spot."

Pro Moves To Remember

- Screenshot directions before you lose Wi Fi.
- Use Google Maps offline.
- Keep small bills for buses.
- Ask locals where they buy tickets, tourist kiosks add tax in spirit if not in name.
- Travel off peak, same route, fewer people, lower fares.

You are not a tourist. You are a temporary local. Move like one and you will spend like one.

Night Travel And Safety Hacks

Night movement is a money multiplier. Transportation is quieter, lines are shorter, prices drop when most people sleep. Overnight buses and trains are the broke traveler's business class. Sleep in one city, wake in another. That is one less hotel bill and one less wasted day.

When You Book Night Rides

- Pick the latest departure you can actually sleep through.
- Choose semi recline or sleeper if available. The few extra dollars matter.
- Hoodie, headphones, neck pillow, sit near other travelers, not isolated in the back row.
- Set an alarm for 15 minutes before arrival. Overnight drivers do not always announce stops.

Stations, Airports, And Safety

- Stick to open, well lit areas, near food courts, 24 hour cafes, or security.
- Avoid dark corners and empty platforms.
- Lock your bag to something solid when you doze.
- Rotate naps if you have a partner.
- Use your bag as a pillow and zip everything inside.
- If you must overnight in an airport, research traveler reviews for sleep friendly zones.

The Hidden Value Of Timing

Your clock is part of your cost. Off peak rides can cut prices 20 to 50 percent, traffic is lighter, seats are easier to find, and you arrive early enough to check in and start living. Always compare the total cost of a cheap ticket against what it saves in accommodation. If a $20 night bus replaces a $60 hotel night, you did not just save $40, you bought an extra day.

Smart Safety Habits

- Scan your passport and ID. Store copies in email and cloud.
- Separate money, one stash in your bag, one on you, one hidden.
- Carry a dummy wallet with a few small bills.
- Do not flash cash, jewelry, or new gear.
- Trust your gut. If a street or offer feels off, it probably is.
- Walk like you know where you are going, even when you do not.

Night Movement Equals Next Level Freedom

When the world sleeps, buses roll, planes lift, trains glide. That is the rhythm of cheap travel, motion without wasted money. Do not fear the dark. Be strategic in it.

Transportation should feel like momentum, not friction. Pick the mode that matches your distance and budget. Use the pass or cap that simplifies your day. Keep a couple of scripts ready for the moments someone tries to "convenience fee" you out of a good deal. Move smart and the city opens up without emptying your wallet.

Cheap Things To Do

Become a problem solver. When most people think about traveling, they picture expensive tours, overpriced theme parks, and excursions that can eat through half their budget in a single day. They believe the only way to make a trip "worth it" is to buy their way into fun. That mindset is not just wrong, it's a trap. The truth is, some of the most memorable experiences you'll ever have while traveling don't cost much at all.

There's a difference between cheap travel and budget travel, and if you want to keep your wallet healthy while still enjoying your trip, you need to understand that difference. Cheap travel is when you cut corners at every possible turn, even if it hurts your experience. That's when people skip meals, walk miles with heavy luggage just to save bus fare, or say no to everything fun because it costs a few bucks. Budget travel, on the other hand, is about being intentional. You spend what you can actually afford, but you make sure you're still living your trip, not just surviving it.

Think about it this way: if you blow money on overpriced attractions you can't afford, you'll regret it when you get home and see your credit card bill. If you spend nothing at all because you're trying to be "cheap," you'll regret it when you realize you missed out on the entire experience. Budget travel lives in the middle. It's about deciding what's worth your money, cutting the fat, and chasing experiences that give you value.

One of the best tools to make this mindset real is simple: write it down. Write down how much you're going to spend per day. Write down what you're willing to spend money on, and what you refuse to. If you know ahead of time that you'll allow yourself one paid activity each day, then when a tour guide tries to upsell you on three, you already have your boundaries set. Without that, you'll spend based on emotion, and that's where people lose control.

I like to remind myself with this rule:

"The key to make your money last is by writing it down."

Not just in your head, but actually in a notebook, a phone note, or even a spreadsheet. When you put numbers on paper, they feel more real. You stop wishing you could spend like a millionaire and start accepting what you can actually afford. That difference can be the line between coming home broke and coming home with extra cash in your pocket.

Another mistake people make is building their trip backwards. They start by dreaming up everything they want to do and then hoping the budget magically works out. Smart travelers do the opposite. You book your flight and your hotel first, lock those down, because they're your non-negotiables. Then, you plan your activity budget around what's left. This forces you to live in reality. If you only have $500 left for a weeklong trip, that means you need to find activities that average less than $75 a day, and there are plenty of ways to make that work.

Here's the best part: the activities that cost little or nothing are often the ones that leave the strongest memories. The free concert in a park, the hike up a hill with a view over the whole city, the random street parade you stumble into, those are the stories you'll tell for years. Nobody brags about paying $200 for a tourist trap bus tour. They brag about the time they wandered into a local market and ended up dancing in the street with strangers.

When I talk about doing more with less, I don't mean being stingy. I mean being strategic. I mean swapping "expensive but forgettable" with "cheap but unforgettable." Ask any frequent traveler what their favorite memory is, and nine times out of ten it won't be the overpriced excursion. It'll be something small, authentic, and unexpected.

This mindset is also about humility. Ask a local what they do on weekends. You'll be shocked by how many free or dirt-cheap options they'll give you. Locals know which beaches are free, which trails give the best views, which markets have the best street food. Tourists pay for brochures and packages; locals just live life. If you can tap into that, you'll unlock experiences no travel agency can sell you.

Don't underestimate the power of travel blogs and YouTube, either. In the old days you needed guidebooks. Now you can type "free things to do in Lisbon" into YouTube and watch dozens of people show you their favorite spots. Blogs are often written by travelers just like you, who want to share what worked and what didn't. These resources are free, but the knowledge they give you can save you hundreds of dollars.

So here's the foundation for this chapter: the mindset matters more than the money. If you chase status, you'll overspend. If you chase value, you'll thrive. Write it down, stay flexible, and remember: cheap doesn't mean boring, and budget doesn't mean broke. It means intentional. It means smart. And it's how you'll unlock the best parts of every trip without draining your wallet.

Free & Low-Cost Activities Anywhere

When people hear the words "cheap things to do," they often imagine boring or second-rate activities. They think free means low quality. But in reality, some of the best activities in any city, on any trip, are either free or cost just a few dollars. The trick is knowing where to look.

Parks, Beaches, and Nature

The easiest place to start is nature. Parks and beaches exist everywhere, and they're almost always free or cost very little. Think about Central Park in New York City. Millions of people pay thousands of dollars to fly across the world for the chance to see Times Square or Broadway, but a quiet stroll through Central Park, which costs nothing, often becomes the highlight of their trip.

Beaches work the same way. In the Caribbean, in Florida, in California, in Thailand, the ocean doesn't care how much money you spent. A millionaire and a broke backpacker get the same sunset, the same waves, the same sand under their feet. If you want to stretch your budget, vacation near a beach. Even if you don't stay right on the water, a short bus or taxi ride can give you free access to one of the most beautiful experiences in the world.

Hiking trails are another hidden gem. In most places, trails are free, and all you need is comfortable shoes. A hike gives you exercise, fresh air, and often a view that no expensive tour can match. I've paid good money for "panoramic city tours" only to realize later that the best free view was a short climb up a hill that locals recommended.

National and State Parks

If you're traveling in the U.S. (or many other countries), national parks are a treasure. For a small entrance fee, usually under $20 per person, sometimes free on special days, you get access to some of the most stunning landscapes on the planet. The U.S. also offers an annual park pass called the America the Beautiful Pass for about $80. That one card gets you into every national park for a whole year. If you plan on visiting multiple parks, it pays for itself fast.

State and regional parks are even cheaper. Sometimes it's just a parking fee of a few dollars, and you get access to trails, lakes, picnic areas, and wildlife that beats any overpriced tourist.

Museums

Did you know there are more museums in this country than Starbucks and McDonald's combine according to the Washington Post there are over 35,000 museums in the USA and they cover every conceivable topic. Buy museum tickets ahead; many museums are free (note city-specific days).

City Passes and Bundled Deals

Big cities are notorious for expensive attractions, but they also usually have a cheat code: city passes. These are bundles that combine multiple attractions into one discounted ticket. Examples:

- New York CityPASS: Gives you access to places like the Empire State Building, the 9/11 Memorial Museum, and a harbor cruise for far less than buying them separately.
- Go City Passes: Offered in cities worldwide (like London, Paris, or San Diego). You pay one price and then "unlock" dozens of attractions over a set number of days.

City passes aren't always the cheapest if you only plan to do one or two things, but if you're a heavy sightseer, they save a ton. The best part? They simplify your planning — you don't have to nickel-and-dime each activity.

Free Festivals and Cultural Events

One of the best ways to experience a place is through its festivals. Street parades, cultural fairs, local markets, and seasonal celebrations are often free to attend. From Carnaval in Brazil to small-town harvest festivals in the U.S., you'll see music, costumes, dancing, and local flavor without paying for a staged "tourist" experience. These are the events locals look forward to every year, and they're often more authentic than anything you could pay for.

Always check the local events calendar before your trip. A quick Google search for "free events in [city] during [month]" can reveal concerts, art walks, food festivals, or fireworks shows that you'd never know about otherwise. Skip-the-line passes are worth it when time is scarce.

Wandering with Purpose

Sometimes the cheapest thing to do is also the most rewarding: simply walking. Explore a neighborhood. Wander through local markets. Stop to watch street performers. The key is to wander with purpose. Don't just walk aimlessly — set a loose goal, like "find the best local coffee shop" or "see three different murals today." That way, even if you don't spend much, you feel like you're experiencing the city rather than just killing time.

Ask a Local

Don't forget the oldest trick in the book: ask someone who lives there. If you want to know what to do in a new city without breaking the bank, ask a taxi driver, a barista, or someone working at your hotel what they like to do for fun. More often than not, they'll point you toward a free park, a cheap food stall, or a festival happening that night. Locals don't spend hundreds of dollars on tourist traps every weekend. They know where the real fun is — and often it's cheap or free.

YouTube and Blogs

Travel blogs and YouTube are free resources that can unlock cheap activities you'd never find otherwise. Type "free things to do in Mexico City" into YouTube and you'll find creators showing you dozens of spots that don't cost a dime. Bloggers often create guides to "10 free things to do in Paris" or "How to see London on $20 a day." This information is sitting online for free, use it.

The truth is, you don't need money to enjoy a destination. Money just makes it easier to find entertainment without thinking. But thinking is the budget traveler's weapon. With a little planning, curiosity, and flexibility, you can fill every day of your trip with activities that cost less than a fast-food meal.

Groupon, Coupons, Local Deals & Local Laws

When you're looking for cheap things to do, don't just follow the crowd. Big tourist attractions will always find ways to drain your wallet, but there are smarter paths: Groupon deals, bundled city passes, local coupons, and sometimes just asking someone who lives there.

Groupon is one of the most underrated travel tools out there. Just like we mentioned with cruises, Groupon often lists discounted tickets for tours, restaurants, and attractions in almost every major city. Want a jet ski ride in Miami? A cooking class in Mexico City? A rooftop bar deal in Chicago? Chances are Groupon has it for half price. The trick is checking the site before you leave, writing down the deals that match your interests, and locking them in early.

City passes are another cheat code. We touched on them earlier, but it's worth repeating: bundled deals like GoCity or CityPASS save huge money if you plan on hitting multiple attractions. Instead of paying $35 for a museum, $40 for an observation deck, and $25 for a harbor cruise separately, one pass covers them all. It's not "free," but it's far cheaper than piecing it out.

And don't sleep on local coupons. Sometimes you'll find them in the lobby of your hotel or even inside rideshare apps. Many tourist-heavy cities run 2-for-1 deals on attractions, shows, or even meals. Clip them. Screenshot them. Stack them.

But saving money isn't just about deals, it's about knowing the rules of the place you're in. Local laws can make or break your trip. What's legal in your home country might get you in serious trouble abroad. That's why it pays to do some research, or at the very least, ask before you assume.

To show you how real this lesson can get, here's my personal story of the Dominican Republic, told exactly as I wrote it:

DOLO In DR

Dominican Republic, me choosing to come here has to be the most random decision I've ever made in my life to date. But I have no regrets. Aside from wishing I had stayed longer, in fact I did. I booked a week stay but met a woman while there and she convinced me to stay an extra three days. She offered to pay the extra so I was willing. My first time being out of the country on my own, and my first time ever as an adult, so I had to learn some things through trial and error. But I got my passport and I was off. Arriving at Porta Plata airport was a nerve-wracking experience. Not many folks spoke English, plus I just snuck a half an ounce of weed into the country. I wasn't aware that it was illegal there until I arrived. I'm cool though, not hard to act like a confused tourist when you really are one. So that was my strategy.

First thing I did when I got off the plane was go through customs. I flew Spirit Airlines by the way. They typically have the best flight prices, so they've become my go-to airline of choice. Once I'm through customs, which sidenote the line was crazy long, like four airplanes full of people in one line, and I'm somewhere towards the back long. Now I'm walking around the airport looking for where to grab my bag, and wouldn't you know it, another line. This one, twice as long as the first, and moving even slower. I'm cool though. I'm excited and nervous at the same time, but I'm ready. After finally getting my bag, I'm headed to the money exchange to get some pesos. I exchanged $500 and he gave me back a lot more bills than I gave him. At the time of my trip, one U.S. dollar was worth somewhere around 50 Dominican pesos, so I was ready for the next seven days. I got outside the airport happy as heck. I didn't get arrested for the drug paraphernalia. In my bag, and I decide to call an Uber. Internet already acting a little shaky. I can already tell what kind of trip this is about to be. Once I leave the airport, I have no connection to the outside world. Scary at the same time. Scary at that time because social media pretty much ruled my life. But I'm here, so no turning back now.

I get into my Uber, and my driver is super friendly, and he speaks English, so I'm happy. Once I'm in, he pulls off and asks me how much Uber was charging me for the 40-minute drive to the resort. I told him around $60, and he told me if I canceled the trip, he would only charge me $40, since Uber was only paying him like $20 for the drive. I thought about it for a second as I sat in the backseat watching the airport slowly disappear. After screenshotting the driver profile, I canceled the trip and agreed. I'm back nervous again, hoping he doesn't try to rob me or worse. I just kept reciting the pull-ups pamper in my head over and over. I'm a big kid now. I'm a big kid now. I'm a big kid now. Airport is gone, but what I now saw had my nerves gone too. The most beautiful mountains and trees I have ever seen in my life. Trees flowing up the mountains like waves from the ocean. Fog so high it could be mistaken as a cloud touching the earth. So much color, so many people, fruit stands and mopeds, food everywhere. In every free, every few yards we drove, children playing soccer and the locals working and going about their day as if I don't exist. And yet it felt like everything that I was seeing was uniquely made for no more. Children playing soccer and the locals working and going about their day as if I don't exist. And yet it felt like everything that I was seeing was uniquely made for. No more. I'm a big kid now. All I could say was, wow, I'm really here.

We arrived to the resort in Porto Puna with no issues and a smooth, enjoyable ride. I actually made friends with the guy. He gave me his number and said, My friend, anytime you need a ride, just call me and I'm here. I'm staying at the Blank Resort. And it was beautiful women around me from the second I stepped outside the car. Adios Mios. Check-in was super quick and easy. They gave me a wristband so all the staff knew I was an all-inclusive guest, which means access to everywhere and unlimited free food and alcohol. Oh yeah, let the games begin. They take me to my room, and I'm looking around as I'm walking. I cannot wait to get started. I drop my bags off my shoulders and immediately take a giant belly flop on the king bed. I could have taken a nap right there. The room was beautiful beyond my expectations with its high ceilings, paper fans, large balcony, and even larger living room area. I felt at home and comfortable pretty fast. So, guess what I did? Yup, I smoked a jay. I had snuck in from America, and I've never in my life been so happy. Once I'm done, I started taking pictures and videos of the room. I even took a picture of me laying on one side of the king bed alone with the other side wide open and posted it on Instagram with the caption, "this could be you, but you playing" as I drew a little stick person lady laying next to me. Oh yeah, I'm paying $10 a day for service down here. I know, stupid and not worth it. I told you, trial and error.

Now I'm finally out of the room exploring the beach resort, and I'm amazed and grinning at every corner from the huge outdoor dining hall to the bars filled with liquor every few feet. My favorite being the swim-up bar in the pool. I spent a lot of time there throughout this trip as I was making my way down the stairs there. I saw about four peacocks walking around free, one of them spreading its feathers big and wide for a female peacock. I'm in a happy place right now. I'm walking the beach, I didn't bring flip-flops, so there's sand and my New Balance 808s. Again, I say trial and error, but oh my goodness, it's so beautiful, glorious even. I look out on the ocean and the water is a blue as the eye can see, slowly merging with the blueness of the sky up close, clear with some seaweed and seashells visible underneath. As I'm walking, I see families enjoying their time together, people in boats, locals walking with coconuts and kayaks with the paddles strapped to them. The beach goes on for what seems like forever. I see beautiful local women braiding hair with two or three women on a single person's hair at a time. I have pretty long hair, but I got it in box braids before I even left Maryland. So I would go, but my hair was already done. This didn't stop them from flocking towards me, touching my hair saying, oh baby, your hair is so beautiful, let us play in it. It was truly tempting, but I passed.

In the distance, as I'm still walking, I see a huge cliff with people jumping off, and I even see a water park I personally would be, won't be doing either. Cliff diving is definitely not for me. And if I wanted to go to a water park, I would have gone to Six Flags America, 20 minutes from my house. Regardless, this place is truly remarkable. Now that I think about it, Six Flags just closed down. So maybe that water park wasn't a bad idea. Anyway, I checked the time and it's almost dinnertime. I'm getting hungry anyway, so I'm ready to see what's on the menu. I walked back, and I noticed an adult-only section with restaurants and bars attached. Definitely will be checking that out later. I make it back to the main dining hall for dinner, and I'm loving what I'm seeing. An all you can eat buffet with an island theme. I'm not in DR, I'm in heaven.

The rest of the night was chill. Spent some time at the bar before eventually heading back in my room for the night to smoke. My time on this island has given me a lot to think about. Number one being I need to move to the Dominican Republic. Number two being why am I just now starting to travel? And so I'm so good at finding great deals and have worked in the travel industry for years and helped bachelors and singles travel the world, while I myself only choose to either travel with girlfriends or my mom. This is an entirely different experience. So, anyway, the next day I logged into the Tinder app. I have a few ladies already lined up for me. I went through more trial and error with this, though. I was talking to a girl for a few weeks before my trip, but by the time I was here, I had gotten so many new matches that looked better than hers, I stopped responding to her. Just keeping it real.

I chose this really pretty girl I matched with and had her pull up to the resort. Personally, I just wanted to get straight to business, but she went straight to the front desk and waited for me out in the open. Keep in mind, there are many entrances to the resort that are discreet, but she was smart. The front desk clerk added her to my plus one, which was already included in my stay. So now she has a wristband and was able to eat and drink for free. I was a little blown, but whatever. Now I have a little company for a few hours. She turned out to be a pretty nice girl, and we are still friends to this day. Even though she didn't speak English, Google Translate helped us talk and become friends. I mean, she follows me on Instagram. That's what I mean by friends. And sometimes I respond to her messages.

She's gone now, and I'm relaxing heavily. Soaking in the beautiful island sun, brought my laptop to get some work done, and made some money on the stock market. Things are great. I explore the rest of the resort some more and make my way to the adult-only hot tub, meeting some interesting, friendly folks along the way. One person that I met and stayed in contact with was a police officer from California. He was on the island taking full advantage of the working girls and cheap prices. He kept saying, $40 for the sexiest women I've ever seen, bruh. I had to. He was down to earth and funny. I didn't judge him. Me and him ended up spending a lot of time together. This trip, I considered him a good friend.

The days go by, and I'm living my best life. I'm in the pool with the swim-up bar and notice two women who look like natives. I'm also watching guys flock to them and get turned away. That tells me they're either not working girls or working girls with really high standards. I mind my business. By this time, I've taken my hair out and the box braids, and letting it all hang out in the pool. I swim up next to the light-skinned one to order a drink. As I'm trying to get the bartender's attention, another guy swims up and tries to talk to the darker-skinned one. The light-skinned one interrupts the man and says, Sorry, sir, but you can't afford her. In a thick Washington Heights, Dominican accent, this girl was from New York. I couldn't help but smile as I finally got the attention of the bartender. I told him Jack and Coke, please. Now she looks over at me after finally hearing me speak and says Cuba Libre. I smiled at her and responded with "What's that?" Her response: Jack and Coke. When you want to order that drink in the Dominican Republic, you say Cuba Libre. Then she smiled at me. Her friend looked over and smiled at me, too. That night, she smoked and slept in my room, and we had one hell of an experience. It was liberating. So from that moment forth, Cuba Libre was my drink of choice.

The hardest part of that entire trip was the ending. Coming back home to Maryland after experiencing everything I did was truly depressing yet eye-opening. It sparked all my decision-making moving forward, including future traveling and the motivation, the motivation behind this book. I've had plenty of trips since then and plenty of trips beforehand, but that trip has to be the single greatest trip I've ever taken, for reasons not mentioned in this book.

Lessons Learned

This trip taught me more than any travel guide ever could:

- Know local laws before you go. Trial and error can be funny in hindsight, but it can also end your trip early if you're not lucky.
- Trust but verify. The Uber driver deal worked out, but it could have gone badly. Always protect yourself.

- Flexibility creates opportunities. Staying extra days, meeting new people, and letting the trip unfold gave me memories no brochure could.
- Local deals are everywhere. From exchanging money smartly to negotiating rides, sometimes the cheapest options show up when you least expect them.

Case Studies & Stories

Advice is good, but stories are what make advice stick. When you hear how someone else won or lost money on the road, it makes the lesson real. Here are a few examples, some from my own experiences, others from travelers I've met, that show why cheap doesn't mean boring and why expensive doesn't always mean better.

The Free Concert That Beat the $100 Show

I once had the option of spending nearly $100 on a ticket to a big-name concert while traveling in Miami. Instead, I skipped it and wandered downtown. That night, a free salsa band was performing outdoors. Hundreds of locals were dancing in the street, food trucks lined the block, and the atmosphere was electric. I didn't spend a dime beyond grabbing a cheap taco, and I walked away with one of the best nights of the trip. The lesson? Free often carries the same energy, sometimes more, than the expensive option.

The "Scenic Bus Tour" Ripoff

On another trip, I signed up for a $75 "scenic bus tour" of a Caribbean island. It sounded great on paper: panoramic views, historic sites, local culture. The reality? The driver barely spoke, we stopped at two overpriced gift shops, and the "panoramic viewpoint" was a parking lot crowded with other buses. I realized later that I could've rented a scooter for $20 and explored at my own pace, with freedom to stop wherever I wanted. That mistake burned into my memory: just because an activity is marketed as an "official excursion" doesn't mean it's worth your money.

The Beach Day That Cost Nothing

Contrast that bus tour with a different day in the Bahamas. Instead of booking anything, I asked a local taxi driver where I should go. He dropped me off at a quiet stretch of beach used mostly by families. It cost me $5 in taxi fare, and the beach itself was free. I spent hours swimming, walking the shoreline, and eating a $3 conch fritter from a stand nearby. That was it. Total cost under $10. When I think back on that trip, I don't even remember what I paid for souvenirs, but I still remember that beach.

The Street Festival Surprise

In Puerto Rico, I happened to arrive during a local street festival. I didn't plan it, didn't pay for it, and didn't even know it was happening. I followed the sound of drums into Old San Juan and ended up in a crowd of thousands celebrating with music, dancing, food stalls, and parades. It was like being swept into the heart of the culture — for free. Compare that to the $45 I spent on a "cultural experience" museum the next day, which felt forced and forgettable. Culture isn't always something you buy. Sometimes it's something you stumble into.

DOLO In DR: Trial and Error

Even in my Dominican Republic trip, some of my best memories came from things that cost little to nothing, meeting locals, walking the beach, and saying yes to unexpected moments. At the same time, trial and error taught me what not to do: like paying $10 a day for service I didn't need, or wearing sneakers on the sand instead of buying cheap flip-flops. Every mistake had a price tag, but every mistake also turned into a lesson for the next trip. Cheap travel isn't about avoiding mistakes. It's about learning fast and adjusting.

Why These Stories Matter

- The expensive activities often left me disappointed.
- The free or cheap activities often became the highlight of the trip.
- The mistakes taught me more than guidebooks ever could.

If you want cheap things to do, start with what costs little or nothing: parks, beaches, festivals, markets, walking tours. Layer in one or two budget-friendly splurges, but don't assume the priciest option equals the best memory.

Be the seat, not the buyer. Theaters and comedy clubs need bodies. Ask about rush, lottery, standby, or "seat filler" policies an hour before showtime. You are solving their empty-seat problem. They will solve your budget problem. You will not get the perfect row. You will get the show for pocket change.

Volunteer your way into the room. Ushers watch live art for free. Street races, film fests, book fairs, food events, all need hands. Two hours of light work gets you access, staff wristbands, and after-hours energy without the ticket price. Sign up before you land or walk up early day-of and ask for the volunteer lead.

Audience tickets are free entertainment. TV tapings, stand-up specials, podcast recordings, student film shoots. Studios give those seats away. Search the production's audience page, submit, show up on time. You clap, you laugh, you leave with a story and your wallet intact.

Openings feed you for the price of "hello." Gallery nights and studio openings are public. New work on the walls, artists in the room, cheap or free drinks and snacks on a folding table. Dress clean, ask one real question about a piece, and you are in the culture for nothing.

Proof-of-address perks. If you are somewhere a week or more, some cities let temporary residents get a local library card or day-pass. That unlocks museum pass kits, tool libraries, language meetups, maker spaces, and free streaming of local films. Not the same as "go to a library." This is leverage.

Seat yourself in the lobby economy. Big hotels run free piano sets and jazz trios in the lobby bar. You do not need a room key to hear a standard played right. One soda buys you a couch, live music, clean bathrooms, and people watching that beats most paid tours.

First-class free, but not the airline kind. Gyms, climbing walls, yoga, dance studios, boxing gyms. Almost all offer a first class free or a day pass discount. Take the free class, shower like you belong, walk back into the day feeling brand new for a few dollars or nothing.

Coworking without the subscription. Many spaces offer a free trial day. Pick rain, plug in, drink their coffee, use fast Wi-Fi, hit the neighborhood after with a plan. You paid zero for a clean desk and a reset.

Courthouse balcony beats cable. Courtrooms are open to the public. High-profile trials not required. Sit in for an hour. Real life is louder than any show and it costs nothing. Leave when you are done. Respect the rules. Simple.

Campus = culture on tap. Not "walk a campus." Find thesis shows, senior recitals, guest lectures. Those are public and free. Check the department pages, not the main site. You are there for work that wants an audience, not for the brochure tour.

City from the top without the ticket. Observation decks charge because they can. Tall public buildings, civic centers, and university libraries sometimes have free upper floors or reading rooms with a view. Security desks will tell you what is open. Ask clean. "Which public floors have city views." Take the elevator. Take the photo. Leave no trace.

Too late for dinner, right on time for leftovers. Bakeries and quick-serve spots box "end of day" food fast. Not "walk by and hope." Ask. "Do you discount close to closing." You will get a bag you did not pay full price for. Eat it in motion and spend the saved cash where it counts.

Shop the back of the schedule. Big attractions have last-hour pricing or soft enforcement near closing. If it is legal and posted, use it. If not posted, ask. "Is there reduced last-hour entry." You are not finessing. You are reading the rules and playing them.

Markets after the bell. Farmers and flea sellers hate hauling inventory home. Last 30 minutes. Cash visible. Polite ask. "Best price if I take two." You are saving them labor. They will save you money.

Transit lines as tours. Not "walk on purpose." Ride the longest surface route end-to-end. Window seat. Note the neighborhoods you want to return to. That two-dollar loop replaces five bad paid ideas.

Harbor without the harbor tour. If there is a commuter boat, ride it at rush and back off-peak. No narration. Real skyline. Regular fare. You paid to move, not to be pitched.

Student nights and locals nights. You do not need to be either to learn the timing. Many venues keep a weekly cheap night just to keep the room full. Check their calendar. If you qualify, bring the ID. If you do not, aim for the same night anyway and ride the energy in the lobby for free.

Open houses and showrooms. Architecture firms, furniture showrooms, and developer open houses stage spaces like galleries. You are allowed to roam, look, and learn design for free. Do not waste a realtor's time. Do not be weird. Do be curious.

Geocache a new block. It is free, it sends you to corners you would never touch, and it turns a dead hour into a win. Find one, log it, move on. Now you have a built-in scavenger hunt with zero spend.

Fix nights beat cover charges. Bike co-ops and maker spaces host open repair nights. You will learn a skill, meet problem solvers, and leave with something tuned up. The donation jar is cheaper than any ticket in town.

TV walls for the big game. You do not need a sports bar tab to watch. Find the electronics store with the wall of screens. Ten minutes of playoff energy for free. Then keep it moving to a park pickup game and play for real.

Sunrise is the cheapest VIP pass on earth. Everyone pays to stack into the same sunset spot. Set an alarm. Own the city while it is quiet. Same light. No crowd. Free.

You've got the playbook now: move with intention, buy value not status, and let attention do the heavy lifting. The travelers who burn out aren't short on money, they're short on a plan. Decide your number for the day, name one paid thing you'll allow, and point yourself at a neighborhood that doesn't need a ticket. When the upsell shows up (it will), you won't debate it; you'll compare it to your number and keep your momentum. Cheap done right is not deprivation, it's direction. You're choosing clean tradeoffs: time for money, local rhythm over packaged convenience, presence over proof. You're allowed to pivot when the weather flips, when the line is silly, when the vibe is off. That's not failure; that's skill. Write it down, run the simple scripts, and protect the two currencies that matter more than cash: sleep and nerve.

Stay safe the smart way. Keep the essentials on you, split your funds, know one route home after dark, and keep a charged phone plus offline directions. Respect the laws where you are and the people who live there. You don't need to stage belonging, earn it by listening, paying fairly, and leaving places better than you found them. That respect is a door key money can't copy. When something goes sideways—and something always does, resist the reflex to spend your way out. Pause, breathe, and swap the plan: early ferry becomes a long ride with a view, closed venue becomes an opening you hadn't noticed, missed connection becomes a story with a lesson baked in. The cheapest skill is recovery. Practice it and your trips become anti-fragile.

So go. Pick a direction instead of an attraction. Set the day's number and honor it. Use the pass that kills the mental math, the line that comes most often, the sentence that gets you the honest price. Keep your curiosity loud and your footprint light.

In the end, this isn't about buying more, it's about noticing more. That's the art of traveling cheap.

Easy Moolah

You do not need to be rich to move. You need income that moves with you. Most people grind all year for one fragile week of escape, then fly home broke and heavier with dread. That is not travel. That is a pressure valve. Real travel lasts when your money travels too. If you can touch Wi Fi and keep a promise to yourself before lunch, you can earn from a café in Colombia, a guesthouse in Bali, or a plastic chair at a bus terminal while your flight boards. The goal is not to be a millionaire. The goal is to make enough to keep going, calmly and on repeat.

Write the numbers so your brain cannot lie. 20 dollars a day buys food in half the world. 35 a day buys food and a room in places like Colombia or Georgia. 50 a day turns the cheap country list into comfort, not struggle. That is 1,500 a month. Call it freedom money. People call it impossible because they never commit to a daily target. They chase drama and then blame the math. Do the opposite. Chase 50 before noon and protect the habit that gets you there.

Here is the switch that keeps you out there. Vacations end. Systems do not. If you treat time abroad like an escape it will behave like one, short and expensive. Treat it like a business you run from anywhere and it will behave like one, predictable and expandable. Office life trains you to survive one paycheck at a time. Mobility trains you to build one skill at a time. Stop shopping for perfect opportunities. Start squeezing income out of what you already know. One honest product can feed you. One loyal client can buy your next flight.

Permission is not coming. Start small, stay consistent, stack wins.

Publishing is the quiet engine that hums while you sleep. Books are little employees that never call in sick. When you upload to Amazon KDP you create an asset that sells in Tokyo while you are on a bus in Oaxaca. Fiction, self help, travel how to, journals, puzzle books, people pay for clarity and for tools that organize their days. Keep the cover clean, write like a human, solve one problem, press publish. The first sale notification in a country that does not share your time zone feels like a cheat code. It is not luck. It is focus with a passport.

Digital products are the second engine. They make your laptop pay rent. Guides, checklists, planners, affirmation journals, Notion templates, Canva bundles, teacher tools, each one is cheap to make and infinite to sell. Etsy, Gumroad, and Payhip will take your file and show it to strangers if your title works and your mockups look real. Presentation is half the fight. Keywords and clean images are not decoration, they are distribution. One product rarely moves the needle. Ten might. A hundred will. The catalog is the business.

Freelancing is the cashflow shock absorber. If it happens on a computer it can happen anywhere. Writing, design, editing, subtitling, social strategy, video cuts, voiceover, virtual assistant work, tutoring, there is always someone busy enough to pay you for what you can do in an hour. Build the profile. Set a sane starter rate. Communicate early. Deliver a day ahead. Collect reviews like rent. Repeat until the calendar fills itself. You stop begging a job to tolerate your passport and start running a calendar that respects your name.

Teaching pays twice, once now and once later. Live lessons pay immediately. Recorded lessons pay again for years. If you speak English you can teach conversation on Cambly or Preply or italki. If you make tools behave you can record mini courses for Udemy or Skillshare. The best teachers are translators of confusion. Record a tight lesson on something you actually use, book outlines, beginner AI prompts, short form editing, Canva layouts that do not look like templates, then let that class work while you catch a bus.

Social media is leverage, not a lottery. Consistency beats polish. Share the process, not only the pretty finish. 10,000 real followers who trust you can support a living through ads, affiliates, sponsorships, and simple collaborations. Use YouTube, TikTok, and Instagram to point people toward the products and lessons you already built. Fame taxes your life. Leverage multiplies it. Choose leverage.

If your lane is adult content and you are grown and verified, OnlyFans can be a portable storefront that fits the same income mobility play. Run it the Onlybandz way and it stops being a gamble and starts behaving like a brand. Pick a clear niche so fans know why they are here, set real boundaries so your work does not eat your life, keep a simple ladder with a low entry tier and premium behind it, and use pay per view drops for the moments that deserve a price. Control your funnel off platform with email and text so your community survives algorithm weather. Greet every new sub with a scripted welcome and a pinned post that explains what you deliver and when. Batch a week of content in one sitting and schedule releases for the hours your audience is awake so travel never breaks consistency. Treat engagement like retention work, answer top spenders fast, offer short window bundles when a week is quiet, and host live sessions that feel like a room not a scroll.

Keep it legal and adult. Verify identities, respect platform rules, watermark what you charge for, track income for taxes, and price with intent instead of impulse. Use Instagram for look, TikTok for reach, Reddit for discovery, then always bring people home to your page where you control the terms. Do that and OnlyFans becomes a membership engine that rides with you from hostel Wi Fi to airport lounges, one steady system funding the next city instead of a lottery ticket you hope will hit.

Affiliate links are the quiet stream that never brags. You already recommend gear, sites, books, and software. Put the links where your content lives. Amazon Associates, Impact, and ShareASale pay when a reader walks through your door. This is not a trick. It is documentation with receipts. Trust is the currency. If you would buy it again you can link it with a straight face. Slow money becomes strong money when it shows up every month.

Sometimes the right move is to spend less, not to earn more.

House sitting turns rent into zero. TrustedHousesitters, Nomador, and HouseCarers connect you with people who need pets loved and plants watered. You live like a local for weeks while your burn rate falls through the floor. A good sit makes 35 a day feel rich without changing your income at all. Creative work is not a quiz about identity. It is a catalog that pays back. Music released through DistroKid drips income without your hands on it. Photos and designs through Redbubble, Society6, Printify, and Shutterstock live on shelves you do not own. Create once, sell forever, let the backlist pay for groceries while you explore a new block.

Keep the math boring. Target 50 a day. That is 1,500 a month. Do not hunt a unicorn. Build three to five streams that each throw off 10 to 25 a day. Cover your daily burn with online income so flights and extras come from surplus. Write the revenue goal in the same place you write the spending cap. If it is not on paper it is cosplay.

You can launch from a hostel bunk in one week. On the first day list what you truly know and pick a small problem you can solve in a short guide or a tight template. On the second day build the smallest useful version. Good is enough. On the third day upload it to a storefront and write a benefits first description with clean mockups. On the fourth day open a freelancer profile and send three proposals that prove you read the brief. On the fifth day record a twenty minute lesson on the very same topic and stage it. On the sixth day post three pieces, a how to, a behind the scenes, a tiny demo, with honest affiliate links where they belong. On the seventh day message two house sits and set next month's lodging to free. Then repeat the cycle. One product a week for eight weeks beats one masterpiece someday.

Operations beat vibes. Give mornings to money work, deliverables, listings, lessons, before the world can interrupt you. Put a small marketing block after lunch for replies, posts, and pitches. Spend half an hour at night sharpening titles, thumbnails, keywords, and simple automations. Protect the pipeline with one sentence you can say out loud. One pitch, one post, one product step every day. That sentence feeds you when motivation does not show up. Respect the places that host you. Visas and taxes and local law are not optional. Keep receipts. Track income. Recommend only what you trust. Deliver when you said you would and speak early if you cannot. That is not corporate. That is adult.

When a day goes sideways, and one will, do not throw money at the problem. Swap the plan. If a client cancels, polish a listing and record a lesson. If the Wi Fi dies, script tomorrow's video and outline the next product on paper. If a house sit falls through, line up three more and message tonight. Recovery is the cheapest skill on earth. Make it your reflex.

Understand the difference between luck and consistency. Luck visits. Consistency pays rent. You do not need millions. You need movement. Write the book. Ship the template. List the product. Record the lesson. Post the video. Link the gear you actually use. Apply for the sit. Send the proposal. Your next flight does not have to come from savings. It can come from sales. That is the quiet flex that never makes the postcard.

Freedom does not mean you stopped working. It means you

stopped working for someone else's plan. You replaced a paycheck with purpose. You replaced routine with rhythm. Most people wait to feel ready and age out of their own life. Do not wait. Build small. Build steady. Build portable. When the notification dings in a timezone you cannot pronounce and you realize the bill it just covered, you will understand the point of all this.

Money buys miles. Creativity buys time. Discipline lets you keep both.

Safety & Scams

Traveling cheap does not mean traveling dumb. There is a difference between saving money and setting yourself up to lose everything you saved. People hear budget travel and picture risk, unsafe neighborhoods, sketchy hostels, shady taxis. The truth is the most dangerous thing abroad is not the place. It is being unprepared. If you want to make it home with your money and your calm, learn to spot game before it spots you.

The Real Travel Tax

Every city has hustlers, helpers, pretend guides, and friendly strangers who are not actually friendly. They study tourists like test answers. If you look lost, tired, or rich, you are lunch. Your defense is posture and pace. Move like you belong and buy yourself time to think.

The Classics You Need To See Coming

Fake taxis work the same way everywhere. A driver claims the meter is broken or asks you to cancel the app because he can save you money. He cannot. Confirm the fare before you sit down or use a verified app and keep it on. If pressure shows up, step away from the car.

Fake police show up half uniformed and ask to see your wallet or passport. Real officers identify themselves and write reports. Ask to go to the station together. Scammers disappear when you say that.

ATMs can be traps when they sit alone in a shop or a corner. Use machines inside banks. Check for loose parts and cover the keypad. If something looks off, it is off.

Free gifts are never free. A bracelet, flower, charm, or burned CD pressed into your hand becomes a scene until you pay. Hands in pockets keeps your money yours.

Cheap tours that fall from the sky are a script. Time sensitive and cash only equals bad math. Walk away.

Exchange booths in tourist zones charge pain. Withdraw from a bank ATM or convert digitally with a trusted service. If anything feels rushed, emotional, or too good to miss, it is a setup.

Protecting Your Money Like A Pro

Cheap survives on organization. Split your cash into three zones. Keep a little on you, a little in your bag, and a little hidden in your room. Carry a fake wallet with a few small bills and expired cards. If someone ever demands money, that is the one you hand over. Carry backup cards and separate them. One debit and one credit live apart so one mistake does not end the trip. Do not carry every card daily. Lock extras and hide valuables creatively.

Not every safe is safe.

Digital Protection That Buys Peace

Keep small balances on travel cards so a skim only buys a stranger lunch. Turn on transaction alerts so you catch nonsense early. Avoid public Wi Fi for banking unless you run a real VPN. Being broke is one thing. Getting wiped out is another.

Tech, Trackers, And Backup

Your phone is your lifeline. Lose it and you lose directions, language, and sometimes your wallet. Treat it like cash. Turn on device tracking. Screenshot addresses, routes, and confirmations before you leave Wi Fi. Download offline maps. Carry a power bank. Never hand your phone to strangers for a photo. If you are solo, send your location to someone you trust now and then. Not fear. Discipline.

Secure The Stay

Your stay is your recharge zone. Research the neighborhood before you book. Cheap does not always mean safe. Check locks when you arrive. If a door or window is weak, ask for another room or use a wedge. Do not tell strangers where you sleep. Hide valuables before housekeeping. Trust your read. If a place feels off, it is. Dorms need a small padlock for the locker and earplugs for your sanity. Read the bad reviews. That is where the truth hides.

Blend In Without Disappearing

You do not have to look local. You should not look lost. Walk with purpose even when you are improvising. Confidence is camouflage. Dress modestly where that is the norm. Learn four words in the local language, hello, thank you, how much, no. Those four cut stress in half. Leave the flex at home. Jewelry and loud brands make you a target. Never argue over a small scam. Walk away. Pride is expensive abroad.

Emergency Mindset

Things happen. What separates smart travelers from unlucky ones is the next move. If your passport or wallet goes missing, get to your embassy or consulate, file a police report, call your bank, and use your digital copies to speed replacements. If you feel unsafe, step into a public place, move quickly but calm, and ask staff for help, not random strangers. If someone demands money, hand over the decoy, walk, do not debate. Your ego is not worth your life.

Real Insurance Beats Fake Courage

Travel insurance is not for worriers. It is for adults. Medical bills abroad will humble you faster than any scam. Pick a policy that covers emergency care, trip interruptions, lost items, and evacuation. You do not need to spend a fortune. A small premium now can save thousands later. That is budget math with a spine.

Laws, Norms, And Not Getting Weird

Every country runs on its own rulebook. What is normal at home can be a fine, a night in a cell, or a bad reputation somewhere else. Spend five minutes before you fly and search for laws tourists should know in your destination. You will find notes on curfews, banned products, dress codes, and off limits zones. Do not assume a visitor pass exists. It does not. Watch the room, copy the rhythm, and you will stay respected and unbothered.

Health And Hygiene Are Part Of Your Budget

You cannot enjoy cheap travel if you are sick. Water safety matters. When in doubt, use sealed bottles or a small filter and brush your teeth with safe water. Eat street food where locals line up. Skip stalls with tired oil and empty counters. Carry a tiny kit with painkillers, stomach meds, electrolytes, and your prescriptions. Hand sanitizer earns its keep. Earplugs and an eye mask are cheap sleep upgrades that work on buses and in hostels.

Solo Awareness

Solo is a lesson in attention. Keep your drink in sight at night. Share your location with someone you trust. You do not have to announce you came alone. I am meeting friends later ends most questions. When you walk in a new area, look confident, not curious. Curiosity attracts attention. Confidence earns space.

Groups Get Scammed Too

Distraction is the play when you are many. One talks while one reaches. Tour buses, markets, and stations are the stage. Keep bags zipped and in front. If you travel as a group, name a lookout in crowded places. It sounds dramatic. It prevents drama.

Respect And Presence

Respect is the cheapest safety tool on earth. People mirror energy. Move with humility, speak calmly, and stay present. You are a guest. When you carry yourself that way, most people protect you rather than prey on you. Traveling cheap is an art. Traveling well is character.

Being cheap does not mean skipping protection. It means choosing protection that matters. Every dollar you save means nothing if you lose the one thing you cannot buy back, your peace. Safety does not make you paranoid. It makes you independent. The real flex is not I traveled cheap. It is I traveled smart and I made it home.

You Want Cheap? I'll Show You Cheap!

Cost Per Day: Your Miles Math

Money determines how long you stay gone. Most people will not say I came home because I ran out of cash, but that is the truth. Your money dictates your miles. You cannot talk about traveling smart without talking about what it actually costs to live while you are away. This is the real 2025 math. Once you understand cost per day, you stop asking how long can I afford to travel and start asking where can I afford to live next.

Your Daily Rate

Your daily rate is freedom. If you know what one day costs, you can predict your whole trip. Save 1,000 dollars and the story changes by country. In the United States that might be ten days. In Thailand that can be a month. In Vietnam you might stretch six weeks. That is the difference between vacationing and living. See travel through a cost per day lens and you stop chasing trends. You chase value, exchange rates, and fair local economies. The map becomes opportunity, not limitation.

The 2025 Landscape

The dollar is strong in many places, but inflation and tourism waves reshuffled the board. Some darlings got pricier. Bali and Costa Rica cost more than they used to. Sleeper countries upgraded infrastructure without spiking prices. Vietnam, Georgia, Serbia, and parts of Eastern Europe are quietly excellent for long stays. Plan with value in mind and you travel longer, live better, and spend less.

Cost per day ranges for a budget traveler who eats local, rides transit, and picks simple stays

Vietnam 25 to 35 dollars
Thailand 30 to 40 dollars
Indonesia 35 to 45 dollars
Mexico 40 to 50 dollars
Philippines 35 to 45 dollars
Colombia 35 to 45 dollars
Georgia 30 to 40 dollars
Egypt 25 to 35 dollars
Serbia and Eastern Europe 35 to 45 dollars
Nepal 20 to 25 dollars
Portugal 50 to 60 dollars
Costa Rica 45 to 65 dollars
Japan 60 to 80 dollars
United States 90 to 120 dollars
Paris and London 100 plus

What A Cheap Day Includes

A cheap day is not only a bed. Count the whole day. Food, transit, small fees, data, water, laundry, and the little impulses that leak money. A healthy split looks like this.

Accommodation about 40 percent
    Food about 25 percent
    Transportation about 15 percent
    Entertainment about 10 percent
    Everything else about 10 percent

Exchange rates as a 2025 compass

Thailand about 36 baht per dollar
    Vietnam about 24,000 dong
    Indonesia about 15,700 rupiah
    Mexico about 18 pesos
    Philippines about 56 pesos
    Colombia about 4,000 pesos
    Georgia about 2.7 lari
    Egypt about 48 pounds
    Serbia about 108 dinars
    Nepal about 133 rupees
    Japan about 145 yen
    Portugal about 0.92 euro per dollar

These ratios change how you feel the world. A three dollar dinner in Hanoi can taste like an eighteen dollar dinner in Los Angeles. A twenty five dollar night in Chiang Mai can mirror a one hundred fifty dollar night in Miami. Chase value per dollar, not view per photo.

Comfort, Nightlife, And Movement

Decide when you want comfort and when you want experience. Luxury and value rarely share a street. Ten dollars in Portugal might feel cheap, but that same ten dollars feeds you for days in parts of Vietnam. One week in Tokyo can equal a month in Chiang Mai. One night out in Paris can buy a flight to Colombia. Think like a strategist, not a tourist.

Night costs show a city's rhythm. Vietnam and Thailand give you two dollar beers and ten dollar nights that run late. Mexico and Colombia are music forward and social, with one dollar tacos after three dollar tequila. Georgia and Serbia lean into wine and cafes, three dollar bottles and five dollar entries. Japan is polished and precise, karaoke and cocktails around thirty to fifty for a proper night. Portugal sits in the middle with rooftops and beach bars at fair prices. The United States and much of Western Europe still run on markups, fifteen dollar cocktails and hundred dollar nights.

Mobility stays cheap if you stay patient. In Southeast Asia a local ride is often fifty cents to two dollars, long distance buses eight to twenty, domestic flights thirty to seventy. In Latin America a local ride runs one to three dollars, long distance ten to twenty five, flights forty to eighty. In Eastern Europe a local ride is one to three, long distance ten to twenty, flights forty to sixty. Western Europe, Japan, and the United States carry higher ranges, local rides two to six, long distance thirty to seventy, flights one hundred plus. Overnight buses and trains double as transport and a bed.

Long Stays And Real Numbers

Costs drop when you stop hopping. Weekly and monthly rates flip the math in your favor. Thailand studios often sit around 250 to 400 per month. Vietnam apartments 300 to 500. Mexico one bedrooms 500 to 700. Georgia about 400. Colombia urban studios around 450. Eastern Europe four hundred to six hundred depending on the city. Japan nine hundred to 1,200 for small places. The United States 1,800 and up for the same space. Slow travel can cut housing almost in half and give you time to actually live.

Value Cities And The 100 Dollar Test

Some cities make the choice obvious. Chiang Mai blends calm and cost, studios around 300 to 450 and meals one to three dollars. Da Nang gives beach and mountains with rent 250 to 400 and a fifty dollar monthly scooter. Tbilisi offers long stays with easy visas, rent 350 to 450 and a deep cafe and wine culture. Medellin brings community and climate with 400 to 600 rent and the metro under a dollar. Oaxaca serves food and tradition with rent 350 to 500 and street eats at one to three. Yogyakarta carries Bali's spirit at half the price, rent 200 to 350 and student energy at night. Cebu City is sunny and social with English ease. Belgrade gives European texture without EU prices, 400 to 600 rent and river clubs that go late. Kathmandu is spiritual and cheap, rent 200 to 300. Cairo is history with motion, rent 250 to

400 and pennies for the metro.

What 100 dollars buys makes it plain. In New York City it might be one budget hotel night and one dinner. In Los Angeles a tank of gas with lunch and a coffee. In Bangkok three hotel nights and six meals. In Tbilisi four private room nights and a week of transport. In Medellin five days of meals with a haircut and a night out. In Kathmandu a full week of comfort. In Oaxaca three full days living like a local. Your money is not the problem. Your geography is.

Cheap is not broke. Cheap is resourceful. At home you pay for convenience. Abroad you pay attention. Attention is free and returns calm. In 2025 there are trend chasers and value chasers. Trends drain your wallet. Value extends your freedom. Keep your daily cost low and your curiosity high and you can stay gone as long as you want. Money does not buy happiness. It buys time. The longer you can stay gone, the closer you get to peace.

Traveling Cheap Without Feeling Cheap.

Cheap travel starts in your head, not your wallet. Most people think cheap means struggle and settling. The truth is different. Cheap can be a choice rooted in awareness. You are not avoiding spending. You are choosing where it matters. That is not broke energy. That is control.

The mental game is simple. Stop equating money with meaning. You do not need to spend more to feel more. Some of your best moments arrive the second you stop trying to buy them. People love to flex resorts, rooms, and plane seats with champagne. Nobody cares after the post. The flex fades. The memory stays.

Traveling cheap is not cutting corners. It is cutting noise. You are learning how to make your money last longer than your trip. You are trading luxury for longevity. When you choose cheap on purpose, your view shifts. You stop being a consumer and start being an observer. You notice steam rising off a street grill, the rhythm of a market, the way people build joy with what they already have. You stop needing comfort to feel alive.

The difference between expensive travelers and cheap travelers is energy. Expensive travelers chase relief. Cheap travelers chase connection. One is escaping a life. The other is expanding it. Character grows fast on a cheap road. The bus breaks down. The hostel is loud. A one dollar meal tastes like ten. Patience, resilience, and gratitude show up and stay. Those traits outlast every vacation photo.

Cheap does not mean low value. It means low waste. Every dollar you redirect from an overpriced dining room buys you another day of freedom. Every meal with locals becomes a class in culture instead of a receipt. The switch flips when you stop trying to replicate your old lifestyle in a new country. You are not there to act like a tourist. You are there to live as a person who chose a different morning.

People who travel cheap do not miss the luxuries they left. They gain the freedom everyone talks about. They do not need constant entertainment because the life they are leading is the entertainment. Once you break the belief that money equals meaning, everything opens. The world looks different. You look different. Cheap stops making you small and starts making you limitless. You are not having less. You are needing less. Once you need less, no one can trap you.

Strategic Cheap

Traveling cheap is not cutting out everything that costs money. It is spending with aim. You are not living in poverty. You are living with purpose. Being cheap is skipping life from fear. Being smart is paying for what actually moves you. You cannot run on fear and call it freedom.

Strategy changes how you spend. You stop spending like a tourist. You start spending like a local. Value shifts by country. Ten dollars in Thailand buys a feast. Ten dollars in London buys a coffee and a look. Knowing the difference is power. Good travelers master redirection. They do not save by starving. They save by pointing money at memory. Fifty on cocktails in a tourist bar turns into five on street food and ten on a train to a city you have never seen. Weeks become months because you keep making that swap.

Small choices stack fast. You pay extra for safety and sanity. The better hostel. The reputable driver. The more secure route. You cut back on vanity and convenience. Public buses over private transfers. Wash your clothes instead of paying someone else to fold them. Local meals over imported brands. You start doing more with less and realize you were wasting half your money back home.

Every decision becomes a clarity test. Ask one question. Is this improving my experience or just inflating my ego. That question saves thousands. Once you get comfortable with strategic spending, travel stops being a countdown. You stop saying I only have two weeks. You start thinking I can stay as long as I manage my money. That is how a trip becomes a lifestyle.

Some people travel to show off. Others travel to grow. You can tell by the receipts. One person brags about the hotel. The other brags about what they learned. One goes home broke. The other does not want to go home at all. Comfort is not always worth the price. The sunrise from a five star bed is the same sunrise from a fifteen dollar guesthouse. The expensive dinner is the same dish a vendor serves for a fraction. The luxury is not the price. It is the moment.

Ego Detox

A lot of people cannot travel cheap because their ego refuses. They want the world, but only if it looks good. They want adventure, but only if it photographs well. They say freedom, but they mean attention. You cannot chase both. One cancels the other.

Ego is expensive. It buys comfort you do not need, clothes you will never wear again, rooms that look better online than in person. Ego makes you broke in real life and rich on a screen. Detox the need to impress. Be okay with not performing. The critics are not living your days. Most are too scared to live their own.

Travel humbles you. You are not special because you move around. You are not above anyone because you crossed a border. You are a guest. You are there to experience, not to dominate. Cheap travel tests that truth. You will sit on crowded buses. You will sweat in hostels. You will eat food without a review. You learn fast that comfort and happiness are not the same thing.

You will meet travelers with less money and more peace. They laugh easier. They move lighter. They let go of the performance that drains people at home. Ego keeps you chasing validation. Freedom has no audience requirement. Travel for yourself and the lens changes. You look for memories, not metrics. You notice beauty most people scroll past. You stop asking how can I post this and start asking how can I remember this.

The people you meet do not care about your job title or your luggage brand. They care about your energy and how you treat people and whether you listen. Cheap travel strips illusion. It shows you what you actually need. You stop chasing status. You stop comparing. You stop pretending. Once you stop performing, you start existing. Once you stop impressing, you start connecting. The world gets smaller. Your perspective gets huge. You are not proving you can survive without money. You are proving money is not what makes you alive.

Living Rich Without Spending Rich

The richest people are not flexing luxury. They built a life they do not need to escape. They are not running up bills. They are running up peace. Living rich is not a number. It is how much freedom you buy with the number you have. Some people make six figures and cannot afford time. Some people make fifty a day and live like they won the lottery because they defined wealth as time and movement and calm.

Travel teaches that money matters when it creates experience. You can spend three thousand on a weekend or three thousand on three months. Same total. Different life. Most people burn cash chasing comfort. You will use yours to chase days you remember. Every dollar is a choice. Validation or longevity. Five minutes of status or a memory that lasts years. When your budget becomes a tool instead of a limit, you stop feeling broke and start feeling free.

Luxury is easy to buy. Meaning is not. Meaning takes patience, awareness, and humility. The best parts of life are often free. A sunrise through a bus window. A swim in a cove with no name. A conversation that gets under your armor. No card can buy that.

Living rich without spending rich means you stop feeding drains. You stop buying clothes to belong to rooms that do not matter. You stop eating where prices prove nothing. You stop performing for people who would not notice if you disappeared. Instead you buy time. You buy space. You buy another week abroad instead of another pair of shoes. You buy peace instead of approval.

Life gets light. You stop checking your phone for permission to enjoy your day. You stop competing with people who are not even in your race. You stop counting dollars and start counting memories. You learn how to make a ten dollar day feel like a thousand. Cooking with locals instead of reservations. Taking the long way because it is prettier. Sleeping cheap and waking up somewhere new.

Abundance is not more. Abundance is enough. Once you have enough, everything else is noise. Most people chase luxury and miss that the real luxury is time and health and movement and calm. Living rich without spending rich is replacing money with meaning on purpose. You still eat well, sleep well, live well, and you never have to impress anyone to earn it. Your soul feels full. Your freedom stays intact. Your days stop feeling borrowed.

The real secret to traveling cheap without feeling cheap is this. Joy is not for sale. Learn that and you already made it.

Bridge To The Numbers

Cheap without feeling cheap is choosing freedom over performance. It is knowing what fills you and cutting what does not. When you move with intention, your days get lighter, your money lasts longer, and your memories get louder. You stop chasing views for other people and start stacking moments for yourself. That is the win. Now get practical. Mindset decides how you travel. Numbers decide how long you can keep going. Next we break down real daily costs by country and by lifestyle. You will see what a day costs in Thailand versus Mexico, how far one hundred dollars stretches in Vietnam compared to the United States, and where your budget buys the most life. No guesswork. No noise. Just clear math you can use to plan your next move and stay gone on purpose.

Close the tab, pick the date, and move. You have the mindset, you have the math, and you know where your dollar hits hardest. Spend on sleep and safety, let culture carry the rest, and keep your ego out of the budget. Count days by what you lived, not what you posted. If you keep your costs honest and your curiosity high, the road stops being a vacation and becomes your baseline. Cheap is not less. Cheap is enough. And enough, repeated on purpose, is freedom.

Deals, Budget & Travel Tips

The difference between a good trip and a great trip often comes down to how you handle money. Most people think traveling cheap means cutting corners or being stingy. It really means being smart. Deals are everywhere if you know where to look. Budgeting is about creating freedom, not restrictions.

Never pay full price if you can help it. Airlines, hotels, tours, even restaurants run offers all the time. Most travelers miss them because they will not do five minutes of work. Put in the small effort and you will pay a fraction of what other people pay.

Cheap travel does not work without a budget. Without bound-aries you spend emotionally. That is how wallets drain. Live by this line and keep it visible. The key to make your money last is by writing it down. When you write what you are willing to spend, you avoid getting caught in the moment. That is the split between cheap and budget smart. Cheap skips meals and stresses over a three dollar bus. Budget smart sets a plan, pays for what matters, and feels zero guilt.

Travel and vacation are not the same thing. Travel is people, culture, and learning. Vacation is rest and resort. Both are valid.

Choose on purpose.

Smart moves that stretch every dollar

Turn your home into a ticket. List your apartment or house on Airbnb or Vrbo while you are away. Even a few nights can pay for flights. If you own a timeshare, list that week instead of letting it sit empty. Do not leave assets idle. Make them work while you wander.

Keep housing lean. Rent or mortgage should live between twenty five and fifty percent of income. If housing eats more, money stress follows you across borders. Lean fixed costs give you room to travel often and return home calm.

Go where your dollar hits hard. A dollar in Paris is a whisper. A dollar in Lisbon, Istanbul, or Santo Domingo speaks up. Right now Turkey, the Dominican Republic, and Portugal return real value. Less popular often equals less money. Neighboring cities can deliver the same culture for half the price.

Use points with discipline. Put deposits on a rewards card, collect the bonus, then pay the balance in full or park the cash aside for four to six months. Withdraw cash once to limit ATM fees. On card terminals choose local currency and skip dynamic conversion.

Budget airlines without fear. Transatlantic low cost carriers can be the bridge. Newer planes, fewer extras. Bring snacks, pack light, sit down and enjoy the price.

Time your flights. Shoulder season wins. September, October, and November are often cheaper, less crowded, and still pleasant. Fly Monday to Thursday when possible.

Pack like you mean it. Instant soup or ramen plus a collapsible cup turns hot water into a calm, cheap meal. Compression bags shrink clothes and double as laundry sacks so you ride with a personal item and dodge checked bag fees. Pack more underwear than you think you need. You will thank yourself.

Where to find real deals

A deal lowers your final price. A bundle often groups items so it feels cheaper while locking you into partners and dates. Always compare the bundle total to a build your own. If the bundle does not beat your sum by at least ten to twenty percent, it is not a deal. It is marketing.

Flexibility is currency. If you only chase one city, one weekend, and one hotel, you will miss most savings. Stay open on dates and neighborhoods to catch midweek steals, shoulder season rates, and off brand hotels that are fine at half the cost.

The short list that delivers.

Groupon for attractions, tours, boat rides, shows, and dining credits. Read blackout dates and redemption steps. Screenshot the page and save the email.

NomadicMatt and All The Hacks for curated tactics and card

strategies if you always pay in full.

AllDeals and AllInclusive for daily roundups, resort promos, and last minute inventory. Cross check the hotel site and ask for breakfast or late checkout.

VacationsToGo for the Ninety Day Ticker on cruises.

Vacation package aggregators to test flight plus hotel against DIY.

Hopper for alerts and price predictions.

Membership and warehouse portals, alumni groups, employee benefits, and phone carrier perks for hidden codes you can stack on top.

The three minute test that keeps you honest. Write each DIY price for flight, hotel, transfers, and one activity. Add it. Write the bundle total with taxes and fees. If the bundle is not at least ten percent cheaper, keep control and book separate.

Timeshare promos without the bite. The three night for one ninety nine offers are real and require a ninety to one hundred fifty minute pitch. Get the price, taxes, blackout dates, room type, and presentation length in writing. Decline any credit check. Use a separate email and number. Bring a timer. Be polite and leave at the agreed minute. Do not sign same day anything. Add surprise fees back into your math. If the all in number is not a win, walk.

Flexibility, timing, and flight strategy

Deal stacking flow you can copy.

1. Pick two or three flexible windows.
2. Set Hopper and Google Flights alerts.
3. Save three to five Groupon options in your target city.
4. Check VacationsToGo for cruises or AllInclusive for resorts.
5. Run bundle versus build your own. Choose the lowest all in.
6. Search promo codes and membership portals for one more cut.
7. Screenshot every step for price matches and disputes.

Make the savings goal small. Big numbers feel heavy. Daily numbers feel doable. Nine hundred in ninety days equals ten a day. Six hundred in three months equals two hundred a month. Twelve hundred in six months equals about two hundred a month. Move the amount into a separate trip account every morning. Money you cannot see will not leak.

Red flags that pretend to be deals. Buy one get one that costs more than two singles. Resort fee not in the headline. From forty nine with one weekday in winter. Credits you only use on overpriced add ons. Countdown timers that reset when you refresh.

Pack light, pay less

Compression bags, extra underwear, instant soup and a cup, measured personal item to dodge carry on fees, refillable bottle, airport snacks. Download offline maps and confirmation PDFs so bad Wi Fi does not cost you time or money. Keep screenshots of price grids, fare rules, and final receipts. These small moves compound into real savings.

Three copyable playbooks

Las Vegas in four days on a tight budget.

Target is four hundred fifty all in for two people. Pick midweek dates in shoulder months. Set flight alerts. Choose a hotel by total including resort fee. Grab Groupon for comedy, Neon Museum, or a food tour. Test one flight plus hotel bundle. If it is not at least ten percent cheaper, book DIY.

Illustrative totals. Flights for two people about two hundred twenty. Hotel three nights about one eighty including fees. Groupon forty to sixty. Total around four forty to four sixty. Free extras include Bellagio fountains, Flamingo habitat, Fremont Street, and art at Cosmopolitan.

Dominican Republic five days all inclusive.

Target is nine hundred per person. Pick September through November. Price flights into Punta Cana, Santo Domingo, or Puerto Plata. Compare AllInclusive to the resort site and to a package. Confirm transfers. Add one Groupon excursion and keep two free pool or beach days.

Illustrative totals. Flight three fifty to four eighty. Resort three hundred to four twenty per person. Excursion fifty to eighty. Transfers fifteen to thirty if not included. Aim seven fifteen to about one thousand ten per person and push for the low end with flexible airports.

Seven night cruise for the price of a weekend hotel.

Target is four hundred fifty per person for the fare. Use the Ninety Day Ticker. Pick a drive to port to avoid airfare. Choose an inside cabin for sleep and savings. Plan DIY shore days with public beaches and known taxi rates. Skip the drink package unless you truly use it daily. Pack late night snacks and ask for hot water.

Illustrative totals. Fare two eighty to four twenty per person. Fees and gratuities one forty to one eighty. Parking and fuel forty to eighty shared. Total about four sixty to six eighty per person without flights.

One minute sanity check for any offer. Look at the all in number only. Confirm refund terms and screenshot them. Verify dates and blackout games. Watch for credits that force overpriced add ons. Run bundle versus DIY one last time and book the clear winner.

Scripts that win you discounts

Timeshare pitch. We will not be buying today. Please finalize our promo stay details. No credit check and no financing. If anything else is required beyond what is written, cancel and refund so we can rebook.

Hotel value ask. I saw a lower member rate for this room class. Can you match and include late checkout if available. If the pool or gym is closed, can you waive or reduce the facility fee.

Price match. I booked on this date at this price. I attached a screenshot for the same item at a lower price with the same terms. Please adjust to the lower price or issue a credit.

Ask a local. I am visiting and want to avoid tourist traps. If you had one free afternoon this week, where would you go for a budget day.

Late checkout. If occupancy allows, may I have late checkout at this time. I can join your loyalty program if helpful.

Bundle challenge. My DIY total is this amount. If you can do this amount minus ten to twenty percent all in, I will book right now.

Groupon fine print. Please confirm in writing the total after taxes and fees, blackout dates, and how to redeem. Are there any on arrival charges.

Taxi price lock. Meter or fixed. What is the total to this

destination including tolls. If it is this fair price, we have a deal.

Surprise charges. Please remove this charge or provide the signed receipt. I will wait.

Twenty four hour grace. I booked today and need to cancel within the window. Please confirm a full refund to the original form of payment.

Charge dispute sequence. Message the merchant first with screenshots and a deadline. If no response, file with your card issuer using the clean paper trail.

Fewer mistakes, more wins

The most expensive errors are simple. Comparing headlines instead of totals. Falling for bundles that are not cheaper. Booking peak weeks because they fit your calendar. Picking the city first and price second. Skipping alerts. Ignoring nearby airports and drive to ports. Assuming all inclusive means everything. Buying every add on. Waiting to plan activities until you arrive. Not taking screenshots. Letting a sales pitch eat your day. Trusting Wi Fi for everything. Choosing dynamic currency conversion. Using bad ATMs or making many tiny withdrawals. Assuming home laws follow you. Overpacking into bag fees. Not confirming hours or closures. Forgetting the twenty four hour change window. Using credit without paying in full. Not writing any of this down.

Final checklist and on trip rules

Planning and price. Alerts set and two or three flexible windows picked. Groupon, VacationsToGo, AllDeals, AllInclusive scanned. Bundle versus DIY worksheet done. Membership codes checked. Screenshots saved.

Lodging and transport. Confirm resort and amenity fees and transfers. Message the hotel about early check in or late checkout. For cruises, lock parking, port plan, and taxi fare estimates.

Money and documents. Daily savings moved to the trip account. Local currency plan and no DCC plan set. Offline copies of passports, visas, reservations, and QR codes.

Tech and offline ready. Download maps and translation. Save PDFs of Groupons and confirmations. eSIM or roaming set. Power bank charged.

Packing and fees. Compression bags, extra underwear, instant soup, measured personal item, refillable bottle, airport snacks.

Seven day countdown.
    Seven days out, price check and rebook if rules allow.
    Six days, message the hotel about check in and amenity closures.
    Five days, screenshot everything again and print PDFs.
    Four days, currency and law check and ATM plan set.
    Three days, free first itinerary with one paid highlight per day.
    Two days, pack and weigh and move daily cash to your wallet.

One day, reconfirm flights, transfers, first night plan, and charge devices.

On trip money rules. Start each day with something free. One paid highlight max. Ask a local each morning for a cheap plan. Glance at your daily cap before dinner. Keep screenshots ready for disputes. Pay in local currency. Enjoy the moment. The goal was never to spend nothing. The goal was to spend right.

Travel Cheaper, Live Richer

Let's land this plane. If you've made it here, you already know the game: travel isn't expensive, undisciplined travel is. When you stack smart timing, flexible dates, value-focused destinations, and a written budget, you stop guessing and start winning. This conclusion isn't a recap for the sake of recapping. It's a final, practical push so you actually use what's in this book on your next trip.

What actually saves you money (in the real world)

- Write it down. The most powerful tool in this book is still a note in your phone: daily cap, top priorities, deal links, and screenshots. No plan = impulse buys.
- Be flexible. If you can move by a week or fly mid-week, you unlock the cheapest fares and quieter hotels. Shoulder season (September–November, and again in late spring) is your best friend.
- Chase value cities. Go where your money stretches: Turkey, Dominican Republic, Portugal, and similar. "Less popular = less money" is a rule that keeps paying you back.

- Deals > bundles. Bundles feel cheap because they're shiny and "all set." Real deals lower the final number. Run the 3-minute math every time.
- Ask locals. The most memorable days are often free: parks, beaches, viewpoints, markets, festivals. You don't need a $99 excursion to feel something.
- Screenshots win disputes. Keep proof of fares, fees, and inclusions. When something changes, the traveler with receipts gets the refund.
- Know the laws. Learn from my DOLO NDR story, don't assume your home rules travel with you. Five minutes of research can save a trip.

Choose control over convenience

Convenience is the quiet tax on travelers. A bundle might shave five minutes off your booking, but it can lock you into mediocre hotels, long connections, or tours you wouldn't have chosen if you were paying attention. Control is a currency. Keep it when the math doesn't clearly favor the bundle. If a package isn't at least 10–20% cheaper than booking yourself, take the freedom.

Control also means picking drive-to cruise ports when airfare spikes, flying from a cheaper nearby airport, or booking an inside cabin on a cruise because you'll be out enjoying the ship anyway. It's not about deprivation. It's about putting money where it matters and refusing to pay for vibes you don't need.

Your four-part playbook (tattoo this on your notes app)

1. Alert first. Before you choose dates, set Hopper + Google Flights alerts on two or three windows. Let the price drops come to you.
2. Deal sweep. Scan Groupon for the city; VacationstoGo's 90-Day Ticker for cruises; AllDeals + AllInclusive for hotels/resorts; and your membership portals for hidden discounts.
3. Bundle test. DIY total vs. package total. If the package doesn't win by 10–20%, keep control.
4. Daily cap. Decide one paid highlight max per day (if any). Fill the rest with free anchors: a walkable neighborhood, a park/beach, a sunset viewpoint, a free event.

Keep your energy for the memories, not the money

I want you to come home relaxed, not stressed about a vacation you're still paying for. That starts at home: keep housing between 25–50% of your income so trips don't feel like a gamble. When you're away, pack the quiet savers: compression bags (to dodge bag fees), extra underwear (because laundry finds you), ramen or instant soup (ask for hot water), refillable bottle, and a snack stash. None of that is glamorous. All of it is freedom.

On cruises, remember what we learned the hard way: a great line like Carnival can deliver astonishing value when you're flexible and watch your email for those post-sailing thank-you offers ($300–$400 seven-day deals are real). A bad fit can waste your time with slow-rolled "weather" excuses and upsells. You don't have to swear off cruising, just pick smarter, read recent reviews, and DIY your shore days.

The "one week from now" challenge

Most people close a book and wait "for the right time." That's how plans die. Give yourself a tiny deadline:

- Within 7 days, set three flight alerts, save five Groupon options for a city that interests you, and pick two possible travel windows within the next six months.
- Within 14 days, run the bundle test on one package you find and one DIY build. Screenshot both.
- Within 30 days, book something, anything even, if it's a cheap weekend in a nearby city or a drive-to port cruise. Momentum beats perfection.

If you want a script for accountability, use this: "I'm saving $10/day for 45 days to fund a $450 getaway. I'll book by [date]." Put it in a text to a friend who will ask if you did it.

Travel code I live by

- Free first. Every day starts with something that costs nothing.
- One splurge, max. If you pay for a highlight today, tomorrow leans free.
- Proof over promises. If a deal sounds wild, it should survive screenshots and fine print.
- Local currency. Always decline dynamic currency conversion.
- Polite and specific. Ask for upgrades, late checkout, fee waivers. Closed amenities? Request adjustments.
- No debt for travel. Rewards are fine if you pay in full. Otherwise, cash > points every time.

If you forget everything else, remember this

Write your plan. Stay flexible. Go where your money stretches. Ask locals. Keep receipts. And don't mistake expensive for memorable. The best travel stories rarely come with a big price tag, they come from saying yes to the right things and no to the noise.

The First 100 Days: Turn the Playbook into Trips

Reading is step one. Doing is step two. This 100-day plan turns the ideas you highlighted into automatic habits and real tickets in your inbox. Treat it like a gym program: small reps, consistent gains, no heroics.

Days 1–7 — Set the table

- Pick your windows. Choose three possible travel windows over the next 12 months: one weekend, one 4–5 day trip, one 7–10 day trip. Make them flexible by at least ±3 days.
- Turn on alerts. Set Hopper and Google Flights alerts for each window and at least two nearby airports. Add one international "value city" (Turkey, DR, Portugal, etc.).
- Start the Trip account. Move your first transfer today: $5–$15. Automate it daily. Money you don't see, you don't spend.
- Deal bookmarks. Create a "Deals" folder on your phone: Groupon city pages, VacationstoGo 90-Day Ticker, AllDeals, AllInclusive, plus any employer/warehouse portals.
- Screenshot policy. Decide where your receipts live (Drive/Notes/Photos). Make a "Travel Receipts" album and save a dummy screenshot so you can find it later in two taps.

Days 8–21 — Build the muscles

- Run the bundle test. Price one real package and one DIY build for your top trip window. Compare all-in totals. If the bundle isn't at least 10–20% cheaper, go DIY.
- Pick five cheap anchors. For two of your target cities, list five free or low-cost anchors: park, market, viewpoint, local neighborhood, seasonal event.
- Ask a local (early). DM or comment on a creator in that city: "If you had one free afternoon this week, where would you

155

go?" Save the response to your notes.

- Prep your scripts. Copy the timeshare, fee-waiver, and price-match scripts from Chapter 7 into your phone. Edit them into your voice so they're ready on the spot.
- Book something small. A bus to the next city, a same-day museum free night, a cheap room on a shoulder-season date. Momentum matters.

Days 22–45 — Make it real

- Lock one flight. Use your alerts to pounce on a mid-week fare. Book direct when possible, set a 20-hour reminder for the 24-hour grace window.
- Hold the room. Book a cancellable hotel or all-inclusive with a clear refund policy. Screenshot the rate. Set a calendar check every two weeks to re-price and rebook if lower.
- Save three Groupons. Pick one attraction, one dining credit, one tour. Confirm fine print in writing if needed.
- Cruise watchlist. Even if you're not sailing yet, check VTG's Ticker once a week for pricing instincts. When a post-cruise thank-you email hits your inbox one day, you'll know if it's gold.

Days 46–75 — Sharpen and stack

- Timeshare seminar litmus test. If a $199 promo tempts you, run the checklist: written terms, no credit pull, timed presentation, real savings after fees. If it fails, skip without FOMO.
- Currency & law check. For your next destination, confirm exchange rate, DCC traps, ATM partners, local rules (drugs, alcohol, visas). Five minutes now beats hours of headache later.
- Pack for fees. Measure your personal-item bag, add compression cubes, stash ramen/instant soup and a collapsible cup. Start a "don't forget" note: passport, eSIM, power bank.
- Free-first itineraries. Sketch two day-plans per city that start with free anchors. Cap yourself at one paid highlight, max.

Days 76–100 — Execute and reflect

- Confirm & print. Save PDFs of tickets, hotel/cabin confirmations, shuttle instructions, and Groupon vouchers. Download offline maps and translation. Test your eSIM or roaming.
- Fee audits. Message the hotel about any closed amenities and request a perk or fee reduction before arrival. For cruises, confirm parking/port plan and taxi fare estimates.
- Travel, then review. After the trip, log what worked: which alerts paid off, which scripts got a "yes," what you overpacked, where you overspent. Add one rule to your playbook.

- Plan the next 100. Put two new windows on the calendar and keep the saving automation running. Your travel life compounds when you never stop the small reps.

Gratitude & Acknowledgments

This book was powered by curiosity, mistakes, and the kind of people who make the road feel like home. To the locals who answered my questions and steered me away from tourist traps, thank you for sharing your cities, your beaches, your markets, your favorite cheap eats. To the crew members and staff who treated me like family even when I was just passing through: you turned ordinary days into stories worth retelling.

To Carnival Cruise Line for making big-ship travel feel accessible and fun, and for those wild post-sailing emails that prove great deals still exist if you're paying attention. To the folks at MSC who reminded me, sometimes harshly, that service, honesty, and follow-through matter as much as a glossy lobby. Both experiences taught me something I can pass to you.

To the creators and travelers who publish their wins and losses online, bloggers, YouTubers, and everyday people dropping tips in the comments, your free knowledge saves strangers real money. To friends, family, and the unexpected people you meet on the way, the driver who becomes a contact, the bartender who teaches you to order a Cuba Libre correctly, the stranger who convinces you to extend your stay and makes sure you're taken care of, your generosity is the part of travel that no website can sell.

Most of all, to you, the reader. You trusted me with your time and your plans. If these pages moved you from "someday" to "booked," that's the only review I need. Travel cheaper, live richer, and pass it on: tell someone else how you did it so their first leap is easier than yours.

What I Want You to Remember

- Cheap isn't stingy, it's strategic. Spend where it matters, skip what doesn't.
- Flexibility beats loyalty. Move a date, switch an airport, pick the value city.
- Proof wins. Keep screenshots, receipts, and written terms.
- The daily habit is everything. Save a little every day and trips stop feeling "expensive."
- Ask, politely. Upgrades, late checkout, waived fees—more yeses than you think.
- Free first. Start each day with a free anchor and add one paid highlight at most.

Pack curiosity, not anxiety. Come back with stories you're proud to tell—and with money still in your account. What's the best time to plant a tree? Thirty years ago. Second best? Right now. Last question. When is the best time to travel?... Enjoy...

About the Author

LaTrè is an international artist and author from Maryland who believes access beats excuses. He learned the craft of budget travel as a kid on Carnival sailings with his mother and never stopped optimizing routes, seasons, and costs. Today he leads Midnite Dakota Publishing and creates straight talking guides that turn small budgets into real adventures. His work mixes real world examples, checklists, and cost breakdowns so readers can book smarter, move safer, and enjoy more.

www.ingramcontent.com/pod-product-compliance
Lightning Source LLC
Chambersburg PA
CBHW051837090426
42736CB00011B/1846